Steep Creeks
of
New England

A Paddler's Guide

29 Class V Runs for the
Experienced Whitewater Enthusiast

by
Greg & Sue Hanlon

New England Cartographics
1999

Cover photo by Scott Underhill

Copyright   1999 by Greg and Sue Hanlon

Published by   New England Cartographics
                 P.O. Box 9369, North Amherst MA 01059

Printed in the United States of America
First Printing, 1999

Library of Congress Catalog Card Number 99-62719
ISBN 1-889787-05-1

Text by Greg and Sue Hanlon
Photographs by Scott Underhill
Maps created with software by MAPTECH, Inc.

**Outdoor activities are an assumed risk sport. This book cannot
take the place of appropriate instruction for paddling or lifesaving
techniques. While efforts have been made to make this book an
accurate guide, it is the ultimate responsibility of paddlers to judge
their own abilities and to act accordingly.**

---

10 9 8 7 6 5 4 3 2 1   03 02 01 00 99

Publisher's Cataloging-in-publication

Hanlon, Greg.
        Steep creeks of New England / by Greg and Sue Hanlon.
        144 p.   cm.
        Includes maps and bibliography.
        ISBN 1-889787-05-1
        1. Whitewater canoeing.   2. Kayaking.   3. Rivers--New England.
        I. Title.
        797.122

Dedicated to Chuck Kern,
our friend and partner in adventure.

We welcome comments or corrections to this book.
Please send them to:
New England Cartographics
P.O. Box 9369, North Amherst MA 01059

Table of Contents

* Number of asterisks indicate the quality of each run. See page 8 for details.

* Number of asterisks indicate the quality of each run. See page 8 for details.

About the Authors

Greg Hanlon has been researching, exploring, and paddling rivers and streams in New England for over 20 years. He has enjoyed paddling in all seasons and at a wide variety of water levels. Over the years, Greg has carefully recorded his runs and studied the water levels relative to each run. He used this data, along with his own personal experience, to write this book. Like other local paddlers, Greg believes New England has some of the best steep-creek boating found anywhere. For the last 10 years, Greg has worked as a hydraulic engineer for the Army Corps of Engineers. In this position, he has regulated flood control dams and reservoirs throughout New England. He has also played a significant role in designing and installing hydrologic and meteorologic real-time data collection systems. These systems transmit hydrologic information over weather satellites, making this data available on the Internet. This work experience, along with hundreds of paddling trips throughout New England, has given Greg an in-depth knowledge of the dynamic steep creeks included in this book.

Greg's knowledge and interest in the outdoors extends beyond paddling, as he is also an avid climber, mountain biker, and hang glider pilot. These activities have allowed him to gain an intimate knowledge of the region even when the rivers are dry. Greg has a passion for the outdoors and the sport of kayaking. He truly wants to share this information with others so they can join him on the rivers.

Co-author Sue Hanlon has joined Greg on many kayaking trips, although most of her time is spent hiking, running, and cycling while Greg paddles the rivers. She knows many of these rivers only from their banks, but looks forward to paddling more of them as her skills progress. Her love of kayaking and her desire to share this activity with Greg have allowed her to write this book with him.

Preface

As a whitewater enthusiast, you know that paddling can provide endless days of enjoyment and adventure. It can take you to far-away places and remote areas, some inaccessible by any other means. It allows you to experience the environment via the rivers and streams that actually help to create these beautiful areas. This is a unique experience that only paddlers can appreciate and one that is greatly enhanced by the excitement of running challenging rivers with good friends.

This is not to say that paddling is without its hardships. There can be long portages, frustrating bushwacks, all-night drives, ice cold water, and dreaded swims, but these can make the experience all the more challenging. To keep coming back to the rivers, in spite of these sometimes less-than-desirable aspects, shows a true love and commitment to the sport of whitewater paddling.

As we all know, whitewater paddling is a potentially dangerous activity. Our safety on the river relies on our use of adequate skills, experience, sound judgement and sometimes luck. Please evaluate yourself and each run honestly and take advice from more experienced paddlers. Be patient and build your skills steadily. The rivers have been here a long time and they will be there for you in the future. This guide is intended for use by experienced paddlers whose judgement and experience allows them to enjoy and play in this sometimes dangerous environment.

Having grown up in New England, I have always enjoyed paddling in the mountains of New Hampshire, Vermont, Maine, and Massachusetts. As the years have passed, paddling skills and equipment have improved dramatically, allowing paddlers to seek out steeper, more difficult rivers. Because your time is valuable and the water levels in the northeast so changeable, we assembled this book to provide the most current information available regarding Class V creeks in New England. This compilation of selected rivers is by no means complete, as there are still many unrun rivers throughout the region. The runs included in this guidebook are simply some personal favorites. I hope that this information can help you in your quest for those perfect days of New England steep-creeking.

-- Greg Hanlon

Acknowledgments

The authors recognize significant contributions by the following people:
John Guerriere, Scott Macey, Scott Murray, Scott Underhill, Boyce Greer, Chris Wilcox, and Chris Hanlon.

How to Use This Book

New England is an area full of great whitewater. This guidebook describes 29 of the more difficult and less frequented creek runs in New England. These are challenging rivers which should be taken seriously and only run by the more seasoned paddlers accustomed to steep rivers. Enjoy and be safe!

The rivers described in this book are organized by location. First, they are listed by state: New Hampshire, Vermont, Maine, and Massachusetts. Within each state, the rivers are listed in alphabetical order. Each river description contains the following information sections:

General Information	History
Description	Additional Information
Water Level Information	River Maps
Shuttle	

General Information

This section includes the **river's difficulty, location, river miles, average gradient, number of portages,** and **USGS maps** that show the run. It is intended to provide quick information about the river (basically, a thumbnail sketch).

To assist the reader in the selection of which rivers to run, the author has rated the quality of each river. Asterisks were used to designate the Author's Favorite Runs. For each river, the author noted 0, 1, 2, or 3 stars, with 3 stars being the highest quality rating given. These stars are located in the *Table of Contents* and in the description of each numbered run. They are also listed, along with a map, at the beginning of each state's section.

***	Indicates highest quality run; exceptional drops and scenery;
**	Indicates an excellent run with fun rapids;
*	Indicates a good run with distinguishing qualities;
(no stars)	An average run with no exceptional merit.

The **difficulty level** is based on the standard Class I through V rating system. A description of these class ratings can be found in the Appendix. Because water levels and riverbeds are ever-changing, the Class I - V system can offer only a general model and cannot by itself adequately describe what to expect. The system of Class I - V must be used in combination with other information such as water level, air temperature, and your personal assessment of the river and yourself on any given day. Because the focus of this book is to describe difficult rivers, *all of the rivers listed in this guide are rated Class V.*

The **location** is given as the town of the put-in.

The run length is given as **river miles**. These distances are approximate. They were determined by using United States Geologic Survey (USGS) 1:24,000 or 1:25,000 maps.

The **average gradient** for each river is computed by taking the difference in elevation between the put-in and the take-out, and dividing this by the length of the run in miles. This value is not intended to describe the steepest or most difficult section of the river, but rather to give you a feel for the overall gradient.

The **number of portages** is given for ideal conditions and optimum water level. This number is not a recommendation, but rather the minimum number of portages known to have been made. In other words, if a rapid has ever been paddled, it is not considered a portage in this book. Paddlers may choose to make many more portages than suggested here, especially if they are unfamiliar with the run. The judgement of whether or not to run a rapid is, of course, always a personal one. All sections of the rivers should be scouted thoroughly, as they are constantly changing, collecting debris and running at various water levels. A run described today with zero portages may have as many as five portages tomorrow, or even ten portages for a less experienced paddler.

> *Remember: Be careful, portage often, and*
> *think of those times that you didn't and wished you had.*

Description

Here you will find a basic description of the river and its highlights. It tells where the rivers are located, their drainage areas, the names of some of the bigger drops, significant landmarks and suggestions on how to run the more noteworthy rapids.

Water Level Information

Catching a river at a good level is not an exact science; however, there are some ways of improving your chances of actually paddling, rather than driving for hours only to discover the river is too low or too high. This section attempts to provide you with the most efficient means of obtaining the data necessary to determine the water level before you start out. Most of the rivers in New England, especially the steeper runs described in this book, tend to rise and fall quickly. It can be very difficult to catch some of these rivers at good levels, making the experience frustrating at times. Be patient and persistent. This is some of the best whitewater you will find anywhere and it is well worth the effort.

Many different methods for obtaining data and determining water levels are described in this guidebook, including painted rock gages, bridge abutment footings, metal graduated staff plates, and simply viewing a river from an adjacent road or trail. Also included are hints about the hydrology of certain rivers and what levels they might be running based on other known water levels.

With access to the Internet, you can obtain a wealth of real-time water level information. Such information includes *current flow* (generally given in cfs or cubic feet per second) or *river stage* (generally given in decimal feet). Included in the Appendix are rating tables that convert river stages in feet to flow in cfs for each satellite gage. Many of the rivers in this guidebook can be reliably correlated with satellite-linked river gages on the run itself or on a nearby stream. These gages are owned and operated by the USGS (United States Geologic Survey), the Army Corps of Engineers, and various other government agencies. The gages record current water level information and transmit the data over the GOES (Geostationary Orbiting Environmental Satellite) weather satellite.

Useful weather data is also available, including radar images depicting current precipitation, weather forecasts, and forecasted precipitation totals. This information comes directly from the National Weather Service and can be useful in planning boating trips before the rain actually occurs. This data also allows you to see the effect the storm may have as water levels rise and fall.

At the time of publication (1999), all of the satellite gages referenced in this book were available on the USGS national home page at the following address:

http://water.usgs.gov/public/realtime.html

Many of the gages are also available on the home page of the New England District Corps of Engineers at the following address:

http://www.nae.usace.army.mil/waterres/htdocs/index.html

As of 1999, all remote indicators of river levels were also available from **Waterline**, a free remote dial-up service that allows access to water level information from any telephone at any time. This is especially useful to paddlers without access to the Internet or those who are on the road, driving from river to river. This service is accessed by dialing: **1-800-452-1737**

Following the sponsor messages, Waterline will ask you to enter one of the six-digit site codes listed below. These codes are also given throughout this book wherever remote access gages are referenced.

Pemigewasset River at Woodstock, NH	331173
East Branch of the Pemigewasset River at Lincoln, NH	335114
Smith River at Bristol, NH	331182
Contoocook River at Henniker, NH	331145
Baker River at Rumney, NH	331123
Saco River at Conway, NH	331112
Bearcamp River at South Tamworth, NH	335113
Walloomsac River at Bennington, VT	501178
New Haven River near Middlebury, VT	501158
Piscataquis River at Blanchard, ME	235113
West Branch of the Farmington River at New Boston, MA	251279

You can interrupt any spoken message at will by entering a new site code. Waterline reports levels for 117 sites in New England and over 1,000 nationwide. For more information and codes for other areas, call Waterline Customer Service at 1-800-945-3376 or visit Waterline on the Web at:

http://www.h2oline.com

Their address is:
Waterline Virtual Publishing Corp., 103 Bay St., Manchester, NH 03104

Please support Waterline sponsors whose messages are played at the beginning of your call. These companies pay for this service which, until recently, was not free of charge.

Included in the Appendix of this guidebook are Correlation Notes worksheets. These forms can be used to develop correlations between water levels of a particular run and that of nearby rivers with more accessible water level information. Similar forms were used to develop many of the correlations given in this book. Accurate data collection can save future wasted trips and turn non-paddling days into paddling days.

Also included (where possible) are indicators of what is considered minimum, low, medium, and high levels. These are only the result of educated judgement and they are very subjective. What one paddler considers an acceptable level, another paddler may not. A minimum level generally means you should expect a lot of bone. Be careful of high water levels, especially on unfamiliar rivers. Due to the smaller drainage areas, water levels in New England tend to change faster and more frequently than in many other parts of the country. Remember that a river at low flow can be entirely different than the same river at high flow.

Shuttle

In this section you will learn the quickest routes to the best spots to put in and take out for each river. In some cases, you will have more than one option, based on your skill level or your ambition that day. In other cases, you will learn that a "shoulder shuttle" is the only way to get to the put-in. For these runs, your motivation level needs to be high. Shuttle information also includes directions to the river from a nearby town and/or major highway. Approximate distances and adequate directions are given to help even the navigationally-challenged find each run. With the help of a highway map or a DeLorme State Atlas and the USGS maps included in this guidebook, you should have no problem finding your way.

History

This section describes when and by whom the river was first run, if that information is available. This information was gathered via word-of-mouth and may or may not be accurate. Any updates or corrections would be greatly appreciated. Please send them to the authors, Greg and Sue Hanlon, at 97 Buttermilk Road, Leominster, MA 01453.

Additional Information

This is a miscellaneous category that includes anything interesting about the river or anything that you should know before starting a run.

River Maps

Topographic maps are provided for each river. These map images were developed using MAPTECH's Topo Scout software and USGS maps on CD-ROM. These maps are scaled images of the USGS 1:24,000, 1:25,000, or 1:100,000 maps, depending on the length of the run. The reference maps listed below each image are the 1:24,000 or 1:25,000 USGS maps covering the area of interest.

Those who would like more detailed maps than the ones included in this book may refer to the **USGS Map(s)** listed for each river. These maps are the USGS 1:24,000 or 1:25,000 scale, depending on what is available for the area. They are available at most stores that sell hiking gear or outdoor recreation equipment. They are also available directly from:

>   USGS Information Services:
>   Box 25286 Denver, CO 80225
>   800-USA-MAPS

or on CD-ROM (by state) from:

>   MAPTECH
>   800-627-7236   *www.maptech.com/topo*

13

Author Greg Hanlon, Upper Pemigewasset River, New Hampshire

New Hampshire

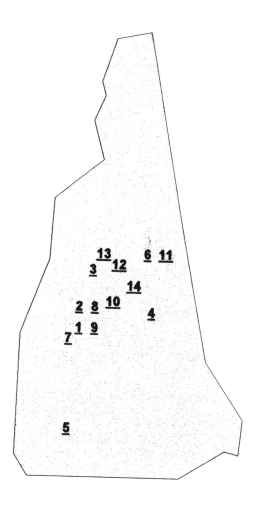

1. Baker River, South Branch
2. Baker River, Upper
3. Cascade Brook **
4. Cold Brook **
5. Contoocook River, North Branch
6. Dry River *
7. Fowler River *
8. Glover Brook
9. Halls Brook **
10. Hancock Branch of the Pemi *
11. Peabody River, West Branch
12. Pemigewasset River, North Fork
13. Pemigewasset River, ("Upper Pemi") ***
14. Sawyer River ***

1 BAKER RIVER, SOUTH BRANCH

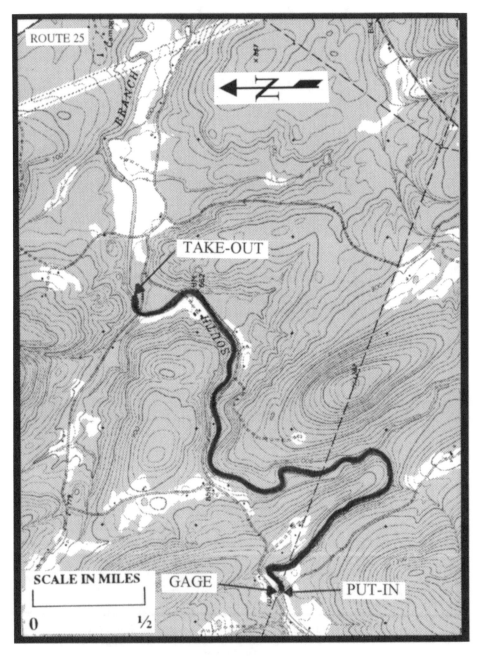

Reference Map: USGS, Wentworth, NH, 1974
Image courtesy of MAPTECH, Inc.

1

Baker River, South Branch

Difficulty: Class V
Location: Dorchester, NH
River Miles: 3 miles (from Rocky Brook put-in)
Average Gradient: 130 feet per mile (from Rocky Brook put-in)
USGS Map: Wentworth, NH
Portages: 0

Description:

The South Branch of the Baker flows into the Baker River just east of Wentworth, New Hampshire. The river combines both steep ledge drops and boulder-filled rapids, making it a worthwhile run. The normal put-in is not on the South Branch of the Baker, but instead on a large tributary of the South Branch called Rocky Brook. From the put-in, Rocky Brook starts with easy rapids, followed by several steep ledge drops before its confluence with the South Branch. From the confluence, you can walk up the South Branch and run the last few ledges, which are visible from below. Shortly below the confluence (200 yards) lies Cannibal Falls. This is by far the best drop on the river. This rapid consists of a long, hole-filled sluice ending in a large vertical drop, which is best scouted from river left. Below Cannibal Falls, the river offers several good rapids and ledge drops. You will pass under 3 bridges. The take-out is just after the third bridge on river right.

Water Level Information:

The South Branch of the Baker is fed by a small reservoir. This reservoir can significantly lag the rise of the river, allowing the South Branch to hold water better than other area creeks. There is no gage on the South Branch; however, the river requires relatively little flow to be runnable. Its level can be judged by the river left bridge abutment at the put-in. The abutment has three small (4" diameter) pipes just above the riverbed. A level even with the bottom of these pipes indicates a minimum level, whereas a level even with the top of the pipes indicates a medium level.

A good remote indicator of the level of this run is the satellite-linked gage on the Baker River in Rumney, New Hampshire (Waterline #331123). This gage lies below the confluence of the Baker and the South Branch of the Baker. Levels of 2.7 feet (800 cfs) and 3.5 feet (1200 cfs) usually correspond to minimum and medium levels respectively. The mean monthly flow for April at the Rumney Gage is 874 cfs, a very runnable level (see Appendix). Care must be taken when using this correlation on rising or falling levels, because the drainage area of the Rumney Gage is much larger than that of the South Branch. The South Branch will rise and fall faster than the Rumney Gage may indicate. The Rumney Gage is available via Waterline and over the Internet.

Shuttle:

To get to the take-out from Interstate 93 in Plymouth, New Hampshire, take Exit 26 to Route 25 west. Continue on Route 25 several miles to the rotary at the Route 3A junction. Continue 7.8 miles past the rotary to South Wentworth Road on your left. Take this left, which is just before Route 25 crosses the South Branch. Go 1.6 miles to a fork in the road; bear right onto Rowentown Road. Park at the bridge crossing the South Branch. This is the take-out.

To get to the put-in, turn around and go back to South Wentworth Road. Take a right and follow this road upstream along the right bank of the South Branch. Cross the river and take a left on Bickford Woods Road, where Rocky Brook and the put-in bridge are visible. Put in here. To get to the put-in for the South Branch proper, follow Route 25 to Route 118 south. Go approximately 2 miles to a right turn on Hearse House Road. Follow this road approximately 1 mile to the South Branch. Park on the dirt road just before the bridge.

History:

The South Branch of the Baker was first run in 1996 by Scott Macey, Chris Wilcox, and Scott Murray. Cannibal Falls was run several weeks later by Willy Kern.

Notes

_____

_____

_____

_____

_____

_____

2
Baker River, Upper

Difficulty: Class V
Location: Warren, NH
River Miles: 3.8 miles (from upper put-in)
Average Gradient: 180 feet per mile (from upper put-in)
USGS Maps: Warren, Mt. Kineo, NH
Portages: 0

Description:

The Baker river rises on the steep eastern slope of Mount Moosilauke in Jobildunk Ravine and cascades down to the flat reaches of the Lower Baker. Just below Mount Moosilauke lies the Upper Baker, an excellent, moderately difficult creek run. The drops on this run are typical of other area creeks, consisting of mostly boulder gardens and sculpted bedrock rapids. There are no particularly huge drops on the run, and at most water levels, there is ample recovery time between drops. The take-out is just below Baker River Falls at the bridge.

Water Level Information:

There is no gage on the Upper Baker; however, it can be run at both very high and very low levels. Much of the run is visible from Route 118, making it easy to judge the flow from the road. A good remote indicator of the level of this run is the satellite-linked gage on the Baker River in Rumney, New Hampshire (Waterline #331123). The Rumney Gage lies below the confluence of the Upper Baker and the more sluggish South Branch of the Baker. Although an accurate correlation between this gage and the level of the Upper Baker has not yet been developed, this gage is a fairly good remote indicator of the level of the Upper Baker. Be careful when making your correlation as the drainage area of the Rumney Gage is much larger than that of the Upper Baker. Therefore, the Rumney Gage may not provide useful information during sharply rising or falling water levels. The Upper Baker will rise and fall much faster than the Rumney Gage may indicate. The Rumney Gage is available via Waterline and over the Internet.

2 BAKER RIVER, UPPER

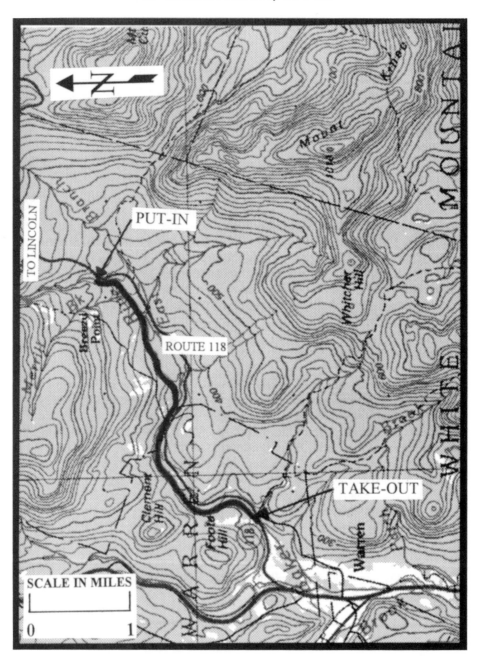

Reference Maps: USGS, Warren, NH, 1973; Mt. Kineo, NH, 1973

Image courtesy of MAPTECH, Inc.

Shuttle:

To get to the put-in from Interstate 93 in Lincoln, New Hampshire, take Exit 32 to Route 112 west. Take Route 112 to Route 118 south. Continue on Route 118 past a road on your right, to the Moosilauke Ravine Lodge. The river will begin to parallel Route 118 on the right. The put-in is where the river is close to the road. For the lower put-in, continue on Route 118 to a right turn where a bridge crosses the Baker River. Put in here. This is the start of the Carriage Road Trail up Mount Moosilauke.

To get to the take-out, follow Route 118 south to where it crosses the Baker River. Take out here.

History: Unknown.

Additional Information:

The Upper Baker, like most steep rivers in New Hampshire, tends to collect logs -- BEWARE! Due to the steepness of its watershed, the Upper Baker tends to rise faster and drop quicker than the South Branch of the Baker. If you plan to run both in a day, it may be wise to warm up on the Upper Baker when the water level is dropping, then head for the South Branch and Cannibal Falls.

Notes

3 CASCADE BROOK **

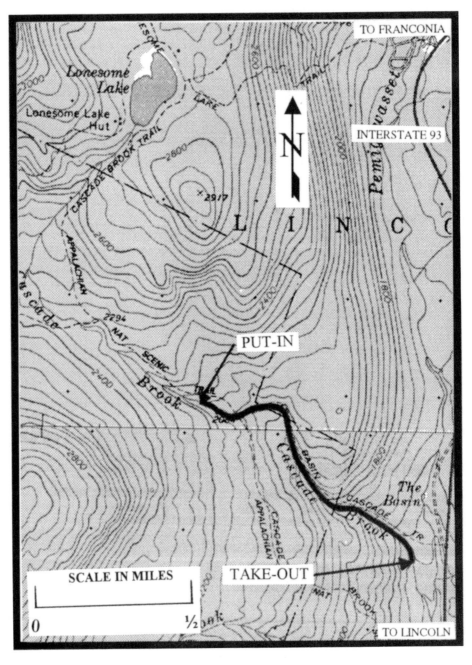

Reference Map: USGS, Franconia, NH, 1967

Image courtesy of MAPTECH, Inc.

3
Cascade Brook **

Difficulty: Class V
Location: Lincoln, NH
River Miles: 0.9 miles
Average Gradient: 650 feet per mile
USGS Map: Franconia, NH
Portages: 1

Description:

After a run on Cascade Brook, you will no longer wonder why it goes by that name, or why New Hampshire is called "The Granite State." Cascade Brook flows from Kinsman Pond and Lonesome Lake on Cannon Mountain into the Upper Pemigewasset River, just below The Basin. This very unique run contains many shallow, steep slides and rapids filled with potential pin spots, making an inflatable kayak or "ducky" the vessel of choice.

From the put-in, the river flows over many steep to vertical ledge drops and boulder gardens before approaching Kinsman Falls. Below Kinsman Falls lies a 20+ foot, unnamed vertical drop, which is considered a portage due to its narrow approach. After the Falls, the riverbed forms a long series of steep slides that are extremely fast and fun at appropriate water levels.

You can take out at the bottom of the slides or continue downstream, running the Upper Pemi to the take-out at the Indian Head Hotel/Resort (see Upper Pemi description, page 55).

Water Level Information:

Cascade Brook has a very narrow window of runnable flow. There is no gage on the brook; however, if the lower slides look runnable, the upper drops are usually okay. The Woodstock Gage on the Pemigewasset River (Waterline #331173) below the confluence of the Upper Pemi and the East Branch can provide a reasonable remote indication of the level of Cascade Brook. Woodstock flows of 4.1 feet (approximately 1,000 cfs) and 5.7 feet (approximately 2,500 cfs) usually indicate low and high levels respectively.

The mean monthly flows for April and May at the Woodstock Gage are 1,320 and 1,380 cfs respectively, a low but runnable range (see Appendix). Judgment must be used with this correlation, as the watershed of the Woodstock Gage is larger than that of Cascade Brook. Therefore, Cascade Brook will rise and fall faster than the Woodstock Gage may indicate. The Woodstock Gage is satellite-linked and available from Waterline or over the Internet.

Shuttle:

There is no shuttle for Cascade Brook. Park in The Basin parking lot (see Upper Pemi description, page 55) and hike up the Basin-Cascade Trail approximately 1.0 mile. The trail crosses the river twice before the river gradient begins to lessen. Put in above a double waterfall shortly after the trail crosses to river left.

History:

Cascade Brook was first run in the fall of 1992 by Bill and Joan Hildreth, Dave Gatz, and friends paddling inflatable kayaks. Courtney Parker was also on this trip and paddled many of the drops in a hard boat.

Additional Information:

Caution: At least one serious pin has occurred in an attempted hard boat run of Cascade Brook. Due to the steepness of the run, the ability to leap quickly from your vessel may come in handy, making a ducky the recommended craft.

Notes

_____

_____

_____

_____

_____

_____

_____

_____

_____

4
Cold Brook **

Difficulty: Class V
Location: Tamworth, NH
River Miles: 1.4 miles
Average Gradient: 220 feet per mile
USGS Map: Tamworth, NH
Portages: 0

Description:

Cold Brook flows north from the Ossipee Mountains toward South Tamworth, New Hampshire, where it joins the Bearcamp River. This beautiful, steep run drops through an impressive gorge containing many abrupt ledges with good pools between the rapids. From the put-in, just above the gage bridge, the river flows over several small ledges called the Entrance Exams, then immediately over Backbreaker Falls. These rapids are followed shortly by the appropriately-named Particle Accelerator, NO_2 Chute, The Abyss, and Z Turn. The run then mellows before crossing under Route 25. Below the Route 25 bridge, a twisting drop named Zig-Zag Man leads to the Bearcamp River. Continue down the Bearcamp River approximately 0.2 miles, running several easy rapids. Take out river right, just above an old broken dam.

Water Level Information:

The gage for Cold Brook is the river right abutment footing on the upstream side of the put-in bridge. A level of 2 inches below the footing platform indicates a minimum runnable level, whereas a level of 7 inches above the platform indicates a high-but-fun level.

There is a satellite-linked gage on the Bearcamp River near South Tamworth (Waterline #335113) downstream of the take-out. This gage is available via Waterline and over the Internet. A good correlation between this gage and the level of Cold Brook has not yet been developed, but it seems possible. Cold Brook usually runs at a level coincident with other area creeks. It is best during or just after a heavy rain as the water level drops quickly.

4 COLD BROOK **

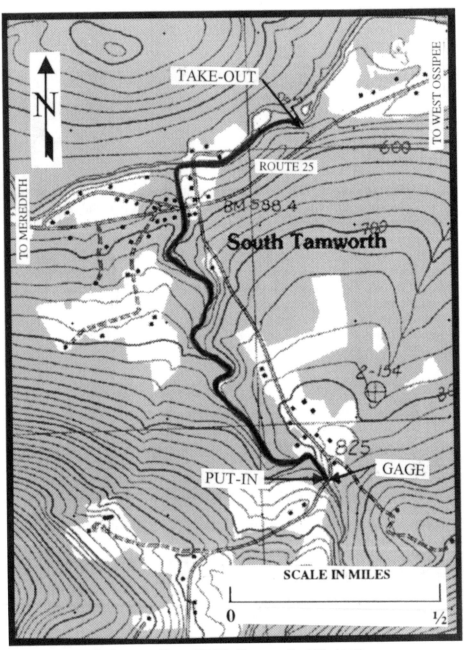

Reference Map: USGS, Tamworth, NH, 1987

Image courtesy of MAPTECH, Inc.

Shuttle:

To get to the put-in, from West Ossipee, New Hampshire on Route 16 take Route 25 west for 5.2 miles to South Tamworth. Turn left on Bemis Mountain Road just before crossing Cold Brook on Route 25. Continue up this road for about one mile to a small bridge across the brook. Put in just upstream of this bridge on river right. To get to the take-out, go back to Route 25 and turn right. Go approximately 0.3 miles to a small pull-off on the left. Take out here.

History:

Scott Murray was the first to run Cold Brook in the fall of 1992 in a borrowed boat, as he had yet to purchase his own. During this initial descent there was one portage. Shortly thereafter, Scott Underhill ran the entire river, including the portaged drop, and Scott Murray decided the purchase of his own vessel would be a worthwhile investment.

Additional Information:

Since the put-in is private property, please get dressed at the take-out and leave as few cars as possible at the put-in. The landowners have been very gracious. It would be a shame for this to change.

Notes

_____

_____

_____

_____

_____

_____

_____

_____

_____

_____

_____

_____

Scott Underhill tackles NO$_2$ Chute, Cold Brook, New Hampshire
Photo by Chris Wilcox

5

Contoocook River, North Branch

Difficulty: Class V
Location: Stoddard, NH
River Miles: 6 miles
Average Gradient: 55 feet per mile
USGS Maps: Stoddard, Hillsborough, NH
Portages: 0

Description:

The North Branch of the Contoocook River flows east into the Contoocook River in Hillsborough, New Hampshire. The North Branch is an excellent introduction to steep creeks, due to the good flat stretches between drops and the river's tendency to hold water. The first significant rapid is Lost Lens which lies not far from the put-in. Several moderate drops follow before the river crosses Route 9 (gage bridge). After a windy, flat stretch lies the hardest drop on the run, The Mill Race. This rapid, formed by the remains of an old mill dam, has two distinct routes around either side of a large island. The most common route follows the left channel. Take extra caution here; the crux lies mid-way down this long rapid and several pins have occurred at this spot. The less frequently run line follows the right channel, plunging over a large, abrupt ledge (see photo, page 32). Below The Mill Race, several technical drops remain, including Liberty Farm rapid and The Cleaver. Take out where Route 9 is close to the river, below The Cleaver.

Water Level Information:

The North Branch of the Contoocook holds water better than any other river described in this guidebook. The river drains from large swampy areas and ponds, which cause the river to rise slower and run longer than most other New Hampshire creeks. The run has a painted gage on the downstream, river left bridge abutment where Route 9 crosses the North Branch near the middle of the run. Levels of 0.0 and 0.5 indicate low and medium levels respectively. The river can be run below 0.0. At the time of writing this book, the State Highway Department was planning to replace this bridge, and will most likely destroy the gage in the process.

5 CONTOOCOOK RIVER, NORTH BRANCH

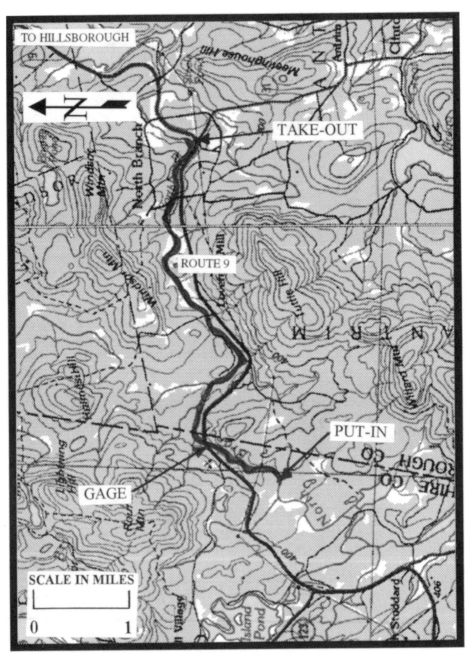

Reference Maps: USGS, Stoddard, NH, 1984; Hillsboro, NH, 1987

Image courtesy of MAPTECH, Inc.

A better way to judge the water level is to look at the drops that can be seen from Route 9. A good remote indicator of the level of the North Branch is the satellite gage on the Contoocook River at Henniker, New Hampshire (Waterline #331145). When the Henniker Gage is running 9.0 feet (approximately 2,300 cfs), the North Branch is usually runnable, but low. This gage is available from Waterline and over the Internet.

Shuttle:

From Concord, New Hampshire, take Route 89 north to Exit 5. Follow Route 9-202 to Hillsborough. Continue through Hillsborough, Lower Village to North Branch Village, where Route 9 crosses the North Branch of the Contoocook River. To get to the put-in from North Branch Village, follow Route 9 approximately 5 miles to a small pull-off. The pull-off is located just after a set of powerlines that cross Route 9. Park by a gated, overgrown farm road on the left. Carry your boat past the gate, down the old farm road, and across a large field approximately 1/4 mile to the river. To get to the take-out, follow Route 9 back toward North Branch Village. Take out at the junction of Route 31 and Route 9, below The Cleaver.

History: Unknown.

Additional Information:

The North Branch is not a very continuous run. The rapids are separated by flat, meandering stretches of river. These sections tend to freeze with thick ice, which does not flush quickly when the water comes up. Be wary of attempting this run in the early spring. If you do, there may be many portages due to long, ice-filled stretches of river.

Notes

_____

_____

_____

_____

_____

_____

_____

Scott Murray running Mill Race Falls, The North Branch of the
Contoocook River, New Hampshire

6
Dry River *

Difficulty: Class V
Location: Cutts Grant, NH
River Miles: 1.5 miles
Average Gradient: 250 feet per mile
USGS Map: Stairs Mt., NH
Portages: 0

Description:

The Dry River flows south from Oaks Gulf on Mt. Washington, New England's highest peak. The river has a large, steep drainage area, making the riverbed relatively large for its gradient. The Dry is not accessible or visible from any roadway; therefore, a shoulder shuttle is necessary. The run can be as long or as short as you want, depending on how far you are willing to haul your boat. On your hike in, you will cross a suspension bridge marking the normal put-in. The rapids under the bridge are a good representation of the entire run. The river continues consistently through large, boulder-filled rapids until the take-out at the Dry River Campground (river right). It is a good idea to walk to the take-out before making your run so you will recognize it from the river. It is very easy to miss the take-out and continue past the Campground, where the river divides into multiple flat, shallow channels before joining the Saco River. Although the normal put-in is at the suspension bridge, there is plenty of action upstream if you care to continue your hike. Also upstream lies Dry River Falls, a large, yet-to-be-run waterfall.

Water Level Information:

The Dry River is another one of those frustrating White Mountain creeks that, although it can be run at a fair range of flows, tends to rise and fall through this range quickly, making it difficult to catch the run at an acceptable level. The river seems to run coincident with the Sawyer and, due to their close proximity, the temptation to run the Sawyer (with its significantly easier access) is strong. Once in a while, resist this temptation, as the Dry River is certainly worth the extra effort. There is no gage on the Dry River. However, the first major rapid (approximately 0.2 miles upstream of Dry River Campground) is a good indicator. If this rapid doesn't look too formidable, the rest of the river is probably okay to run.

6 DRY RIVER *

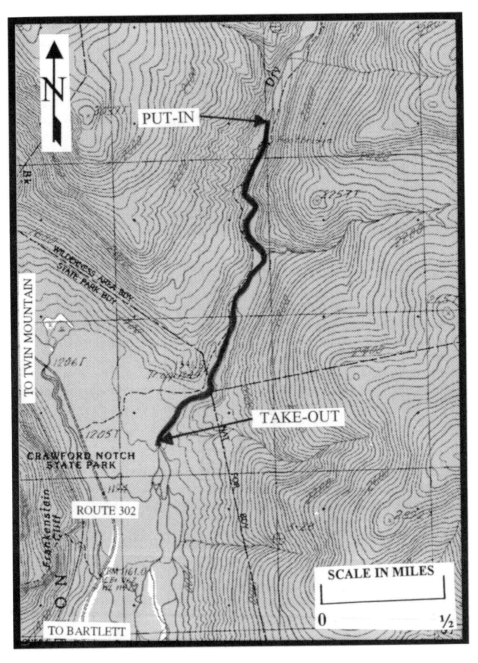

Reference Map: USGS, Stairs Mt., NH, 1987
Image courtesy of MAPTECH, Inc.

A reasonable remote indicator of the water level on the Dry River is the Woodstock Gage on the Pemigewasset River (Waterline #331173). Flows of 5.7 feet (approximately 2,500 cfs) and 8.5 feet (approximately 8,000 cfs) correspond to low and high levels respectively. Also, there is a gage on the Saco River, near North Conway (Waterline # 331112), well downstream of the confluence of the Dry. No correlation between this gage and the Dry has been developed; however, the gage on the Saco may better represent the water level of the Dry. Both the Woodstock Gage and the Conway Gage are satellite-linked and are available via Waterline and the Internet.

Shuttle:

As mentioned above, the Dry River requires a shoulder shuttle. Due to the length and difficulty of the walk, you probably won't experience any eddy crowding. Luckily, however, the Dry River Trail parallels the river for its entire length. From North Conway, New Hampshire, follow Route 16 north to Route 302 west. Approximately 0.2 miles after the Dry River Campground you will see a sign for the Dry River Trail. Park here and carry, drag, or pull your boat 1.7 miles up the trail. You will climb far above river level, making you question your decision to forgo the relatively easy and short hike to the put-in of the Sawyer. Try to focus on the beautiful views of Mt. Washington rather than the drudgery of the hike. The trail finally crosses the river at a suspension bridge. Just upstream of the bridge is the normal put-in. Take out at the Dry River Campground, walk through the campground to Route 302, and back to your car.

History:

The Dry River was first run on April 25, 1992, by Bill and Joan Hildreth, Peter Cogan, and Greg Hanlon at a low level.

Additional Information:

As if the hike into the Dry River isn't difficult enough, the Dry often runs when there is snow on the ground. Snowshoes may be worthwhile to avoid a post-holing nightmare.

Notes

_____

_____

_____

_____

_____

_____

35

7 FOWLER RIVER *

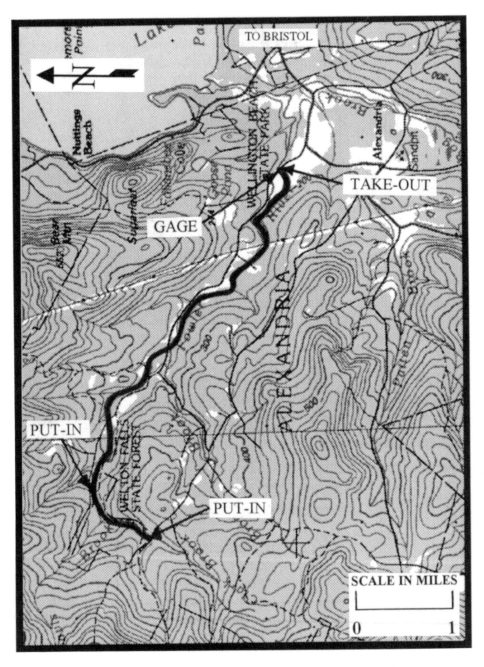

Reference Map: USGS, Newfound Lake, NH, 1987

Image courtesy of MAPTECH, Inc.

7
Fowler River *

Difficulty: Class V
Location: Alexandria, NH
River Miles: 5.9 miles
Average Gradient: 120 feet per mile
USGS Map: Newfound Lake, NH
Portages: 1

Description:

The Fowler River begins at the confluence of Clark Brook and Brock Brook, which drain the eastern slope of Mount Cardigan into Newfound Lake. The best put-in for the run, when the water is high, is at the confluence of Baily Brook and Clark Brook, approximately 0.2 miles from the Appalachian Mountain Club lodging facility at Mount Cardigan. Putting in here includes several interesting drops on Clark Brook.

From the put-in, the river begins slowly with several easy drops before approaching the first major rapid. This rapid consists of two long sluiceways cut into bedrock. Approximately one mile downstream from the put-in, the river constricts and tumbles over Welton Falls, which is considered a portage, and can be portaged via a trail on river right. Be careful here: Welton Falls comes up quickly and is not easily visible from upstream. A good landmark is Davis Brook, which joins Clark Brook on river left, shortly above the Falls.

Below Welton Falls, Clark Brook flows over many fun, steep ledgedrops and challenging rapids before crossing the road. You will pass under three bridges before Brock Brook enters river right. This confluence marks the beginning of the Fowler River. Many more ledgedrops and boulder-constricted rapids lie ahead, including a long Class IV rapid called Powerline. A set of overhead electric transmission lines mark this rapid. Take out at the first bridge (gage bridge) below the transmission lines.

Water Level Information:

The most commonly-used gage on the Fowler is the downstream river right abutment footing at the take-out bridge on Fowler River Road. A water level even with the footing indicates a low level, whereas a water level of 7 inches above the footing indicates a high level.

The run is moderately long and can rise rapidly, so beware of putting on at high levels while the water is still rising. There is no steadfast remote indicator of this run; however, if the Bristol Gage on the Smith River (Waterline #331182) is 5 feet (870 cfs), the Fowler is usually runnable. The Bristol Gage is satellite-linked and available via Waterline and over the Internet.

Shuttle:

To get to the Fowler River from Bristol, New Hampshire, take Route 3A north toward Newfound Lake. Just before the lake, at a blinking traffic light, take a left on West Shore Road, then fork left onto Fowler River Road. The first bridge crossing the Fowler is the take-out and the gage bridge. To get to the put-in, drive upstream on Fowler River Road to Brook Road. Take a left on Brook Road and continue upstream crossing Brock Brook. Take a right onto Shen Valley Road and continue to a bridge over Clark Brook. Put in here.

History:

The Fowler River was first run in the Fall of 1991 by Chris Wilcox and several members of the Merrimack Valley Paddlers.

Additional Information:

An optional put-in, which may be better during low water and which avoids the Welton Falls portage, is river left below Welton Falls (see alternative put-in on map). From the take-out, follow Fowler River Road upstream and take a right on North River Road, then take a left 0.5 miles past a cemetery. Walk up an old logging road to the put-in.

Notes

_____

_____

_____

_____

_____

_____

_____

8
Glover Brook

Difficulty: Class V
Location: Woodstock, NH
River Miles: 1.9 miles
Average Gradient: 320 feet per mile
USGS Map: Woodstock, NH
Portages: 2

Description:

Glover Brook is a small, infrequently run creek in Woodstock, New Hampshire. It flows east from Elbow Pond on Mount Cilley into the Pemigewasset River just upstream of the Woodstock Gage. The run consists primarily of tight vertical waterfalls and narrow ledge drops which generally end in pools. Its difficulty remains consistent from put-in to take-out. Be careful of potholes and shallow pools at the base of some of the falls. Also, one vertical fall near the middle of the run is portaged because of the nasty tunnel/pothole, which consumes all of the main flow. Be sure to scout all drops.

Water Level Information:

There is no gage on Glover Brook and the level is difficult to judge from the take-out bridge because the riverbed is wider here and contains more boulders than the rest of the run. The best way to judge the level is to hike upstream and check some of the more constricted drops not far from the take-out. Glover Brook joins the Pemigewasset River just upstream of the Woodstock Gage (Waterline #331173).

Although no solid correlation has been developed, the Woodstock Gage is a reasonable indicator of the level of Glover Brook. The Woodstock Gage does have a much larger drainage area than Glover Brook; however, Glover will rise faster and peak sooner than this gage may indicate.

8 GLOVER BROOK

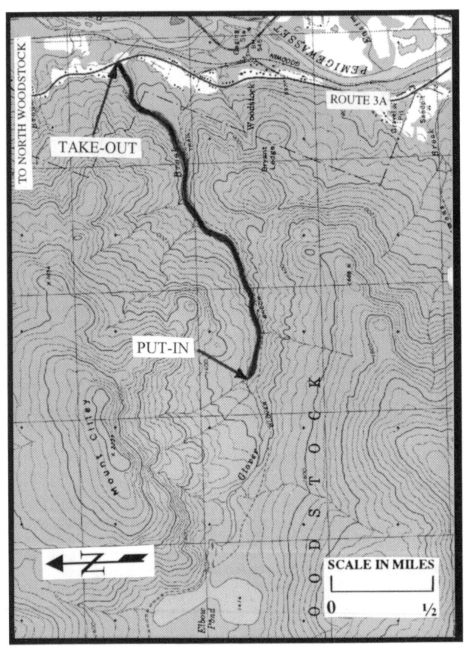

Reference Map: USGS, Woodstock, NH, 1980

Image courtesy of MAPTECH, Inc.

Shuttle:

There is no road access to the put-in of Glover Brook. You must walk from the take-out bridge on Route 3. From Interstate 93 north, take exit 30 and follow Route 3 north for 2.4 miles. Glover flows under Route 3 from the west. The take-out is at the Route 3 bridge. Park at this bridge and hike upstream along river right, crossing to river left. The Glover Brook trail follows the river from Elbow Pond to Route 3, mostly on river right (see map). There is also a trail along the left bank that goes partially up the river.

History:

Glover Brook was first run on April 27, 1993, by Scott Murray and Greg Hanlon.

Notes

_____

_____

_____

_____

_____

_____

_____

_____

_____

_____

_____

_____

_____

_____

_____

_____

_____

9 HALLS BROOK **

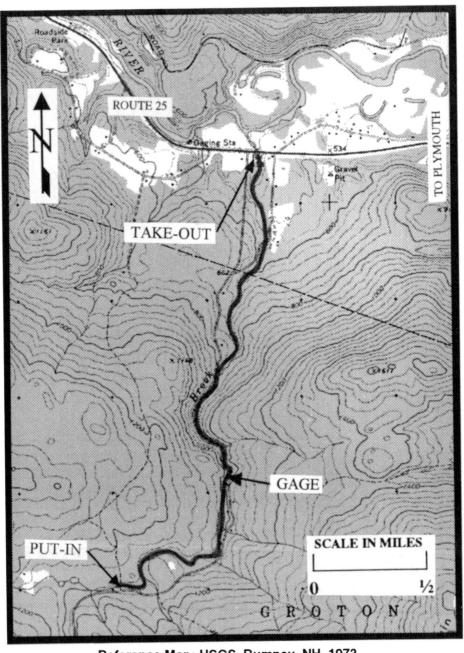

Reference Map: USGS, Rumney, NH, 1973
Image courtesy of MAPTECH, Inc.

9
Halls Brook **

Difficulty: Class V
Location: Groton, NH
River Miles: 2.6 miles
Average Gradient: 220 feet per mile
USGS Map: Rumney, NH
Portages: 0

Description:

Halls Brook is a steep tributary of the Baker River. At first glance, the river looks like a roadside drainage ditch, but don't worry: it's plenty big enough to paddle. The Brook flows north from several marshy areas near North Groton, New Hampshire. Halls Brook Road, which follows the river for the entire length of the run, provides easy access to the put-in, the take-out, and many points along the river. From the put-in, the river's difficulty increases steadily until crossing under Halls Brook Road. This bridge (gage bridge) marks the start of Federal Express rapid, a long continuous rapid with limited eddies at high water. Immediately following Fed-Ex lies the Transmogrifier, the Slot Machine, Jacuzzi, and The Swimming Pool rapids. The river is continuous through this section, but there are good pools between the drops. Take out just upstream of the Route 25 bridge.

Water Level Information:

Halls Brook is typically runnable after any significant rainfall; however, the water level drops quickly, so don't delay your trip. Local boaters installed a metal graduated staff gage on the downstream side of the river left bridge abutment at the start of Fed-Ex rapid. This bridge is located one mile up Halls Brook Road from the take-out at Route 25. A level of 8.0 is a minimum runnable level for Halls Brook. Levels of 8.5 and 9.0 correspond to medium and high levels respectively.

A fair remote indicator of the level of Halls Brook is the Baker River Gage at Rumney (Waterline #331123). This gage measures flows on the Baker River approximately 0.2 miles upstream of the confluence of Halls Brook and the Baker River. The Rumney Gage is satellite-linked and is available via Waterline and the Internet.

Levels of 3.5 feet (1,260 cfs) and 5.0 feet (2,390 cfs) tend to correspond to low and high levels respectively. Some judgment must be used with this correlation, as the watershed of the Rumney Gage is far larger and more sluggish than that of Halls Brook. The water level of Halls Brook will thus rise and fall faster than the Rumney Gage may indicate.

Shuttle:

To get to the take-out from Interstate 93 in Plymouth, New Hampshire, take Exit 26 to Route 25 west. Continue on Route 25 several miles to the rotary at the Route 3A junction. Continue past the rotary on Route 25 to Halls Brook Road on the left. The take-out is at the intersection of Halls Brook Road and Route 25 in Rumney, New Hampshire. Park in the small field between the river and Halls Brook Road. To get to the put-in, drive 2.4 miles up Halls Brook Road to a small snowmobile bridge which crosses the river. Park off the road by the bridge.

History:

Halls Brook was first run by Chris Wilcox and Scott Murray on November 4, 1992, after many logs were cleared.

Additional Information:

Boaters beware -- Halls Brook has a reputation for continually collecting logs and debris. Also, Fed-Ex rapid is not an entirely natural riverbed as some rocks were disturbed during the construction of Halls Brook Road.

Notes

_____

_____

_____

_____

_____

_____

_____

10

Hancock Branch of the Pemigewasset River *

Difficulty: V
Location: Lincoln, NH
River Miles: 4.2 miles (on Hancock Branch),
                 2 miles (on East Branch of Pemigewasset River)
Average Gradient: 155 feet per mile (on Hancock Branch)
USGS Map: Mt. Osceola, NH
Portages: 0

Description:

The Hancock Branch flows west along the Kancamagus Highway, draining into the East Branch of the Pemigewasset River. The Hancock Branch is a typical steep New Hampshire creek with numerous ledge drops and boulder-filled rapids. The best put-in is where the Kancamangus Highway crosses the Hancock Branch at the East Pond trailhead. From the put-in, the river drops over many rapids, including Otter Rocks (a roadside tourist stop along Route 112). After Otter Rocks, continue downstream to the confluence of the East Branch. Paddle two miles on the East Branch and take out river right after the first bridge you encounter just below Loon Mountain rapids (at Loon Mountain Ski area).

Water Level Information:

The Hancock Branch fills a well-needed void in New Hampshire creek boating. Due to its lesser gradient and slightly larger riverbed, the Hancock Branch can be run when the Sawyer and Upper Pemi are too high, and when you just can't bear to run the Swift again. Also, at high levels, the East Branch of the Pemi, from its confluence with the Hancock Branch to Loon Mountain, can be an impressive big-water run.

Currently, there is no gage on the Hancock Branch; however, the river can be seen from multiple points along the Kancamagus Highway (Route 112). The water level can easily be judged from the road. A good remote indicator of the level of the Hancock Branch is the Woodstock Gage on the Pemigewasset River (Waterline #331173). Levels of 6.5 feet (3,700 cfs) and 11.5 feet (19,900 cfs) usually indicate low and high levels respectively.

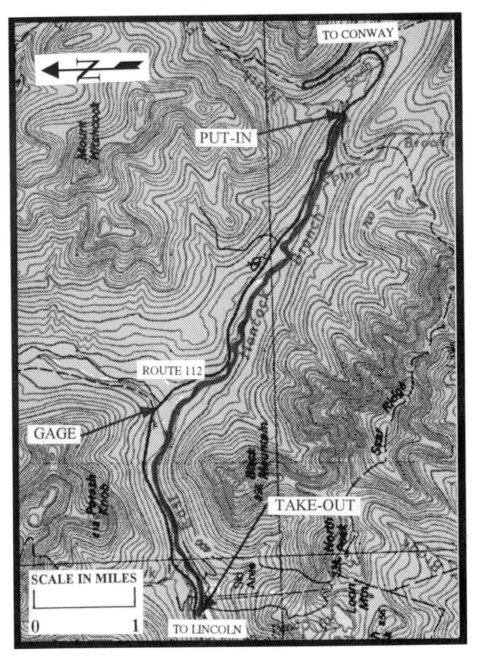

Reference Map: USGS, Mt. Osceola, NH, 1967

Image courtesy of MAPTECH, Inc.

Since the Hancock Branch is in the upper watershed of the Woodstock Gage, its level will rise and fall faster than the gage may indicate. A better remote indicator is the gage on the East Branch of the Pemi at Lincoln (Waterline #335114). A level of 7.0 feet (9,000 cfs) at the Lincoln Gage usually corresponds to a high level on the Hancock Branch. Both the Woodstock and Lincoln Gages are available from Waterline and over the Internet.

Shuttle:

To get to the take-out at Loon Mountain Ski area, drive east for 2.5 miles on Route 112 (Kancamagus Highway) from Lincoln, New Hampshire. Park in the dirt parking lot, river right, immediately downstream of the Loon Mountain bridge. To get to the put-in, continue east on Route 112 approximately 6.2 miles, crossing the East Branch to the first bridge across the Hancock Branch. Park in the Cheney Brook/East Pond Trail lot on the right immediately after crossing this bridge. An alternate take-out is available at the Hancock Campground, across from the Wilderness Trail parking area. This can be used if boaters do not want to run the East Branch.

History:

Local rumor has it that log drivers for J.E. Henry rode pulp logs down the Hancock Branch in the mid 1800s on the way to the mills.

Additional Information:

The Hancock Branch is an excellent introduction to steep creeks in the White Mountains. It is a perfect step up in difficulty from rivers like the East Branch of the Pemi and the Swift, yet still significantly easier than Cold Brook or the Sawyer. Loon Mountain rapids has been altered due to road and bridge construction. Be careful -- this is not a natural riverbed.

Notes

_____

_____

_____

_____

_____

_____

_____

_____

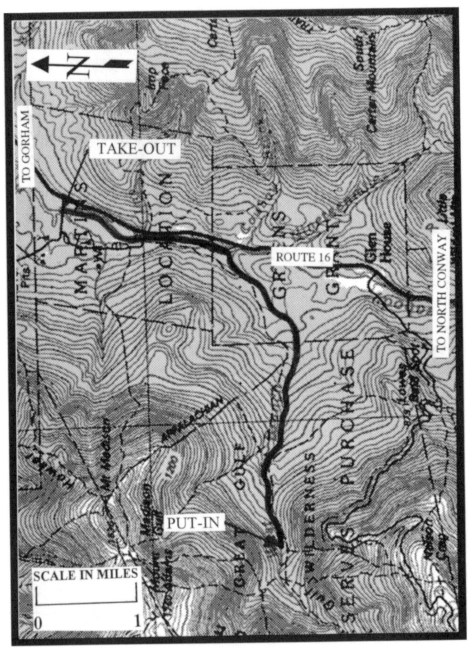

Reference Maps: USGS, Mt. Washington, NH, 1982; Carter Dome, NH, 1970

Image courtesy of MAPTECH, Inc.

11

Peabody River, West Branch

Difficulty: Class V
Location: Thompson & Meserves Purchase, NH
River Miles: 5.5 miles
Average Gradient: 280 feet per mile
USGS Maps: Mt. Washington, Carter Dome, NH
Portages: several and long

Description:

The West Branch of the Peabody River is one of the more remote and difficult runs in New England. The river flows east from the Great Gulf Wilderness Area, draining the northeastern slope of Mount Washington. The only two known descents of this run began at the confluence of Chandler Brook and the West Branch of the Peabody River, and ended on the Peabody River at Rte. 16.

The run starts out steep, but still reasonable, with many boulder-congested rapids. Soon the river's gradient increases and the run becomes continuous; the few available eddies are difficult to catch. It would be prudent to consider portaging this section, especially at high water. As the West Branch approaches the Peabody, the gradient begins to lessen and the run becomes more reasonable again.

Water Level Information:

There is no gage on the West Branch of the Peabody and the only way to see the river involves considerable hiking. The level of the run can usually be judged by looking at the Peabody River along Route 16. Be careful using this as your gage, because the West Branch drains the Great Gulf, which is a large ravine that tends to hold snow into late spring. Judging the level of the West Branch from the Peabody along Route 16 may cause you to underestimate the flow of this tributary.

Shuttle:

The best way to access the put-in is via the Mt. Washington Auto Road which is normally open from Mid-May to Mid-October. At the time of this writing, the road toll is $15 for car and driver, plus $6 for each additional adult. To check if road is open, or for more information, call 603-466-3988. You can also check the web site at: *www.mt-washington.com/mwarindex.html-ssi*. To get to the Mt. Washington Auto Road from North Conway, New Hampshire, drive north on Route 16 to Pinkham Notch. Continue over the Notch to the Mount Washington Auto Road, which is on the left. The Auto Road is a private toll road and is quite often closed if the weather is poor. Follow the Auto Road approximately four miles to a left-hand bend with a pull off and park here. Then, take the Chandler Brook Trail approximately 0.8 miles from the Auto Road. Be careful crossing Chandler Brook, as it can be treacherous during high water. This steep trail joins the Great Gulf Trail. Put in wherever you can access the river along the Great Gulf Trail.

To get to the take-out from the intersection of the Auto Road and Route 16, continue approximately 3.5 miles north on Route 16. Turn left toward Dolly Cop Campground. The take-out is at the bridge over the Peabody River.

History:

The West Branch of the Peabody River has intrigued boaters for many years. Access to the river and the difficulty of the run discouraged them until May 19, 1996, when Scott Murray, Tom Diegel, and John Guerriere made a high-water descent. There was no lack of excitement, with many portages and several serious swims. The three boaters agreed the water was too high for this first descent. Several weeks later another run was made at much lower water. This time boaters paddled inflatable kayaks, but unfortunately the water was too low. The West Branch is probably a better hard-boat run, but a difficult river to catch at a good level.

Additional Information:

This is one run where it is particularly good to have a shuttle driver so you don't have to leave a car on Mount Washington. Having a driver will also save the extra road toll by not driving back to the put-in to retrieve a car. Please keep a low profile at the Chandler Brook pull-off. The owners of the Auto Road would probably not approve of apparently abandoned shuttle vehicles in their pull-off areas. The March/April 1997 issue of *American Whitewater Affiliation Journal* includes an interesting account of the first descent of this run.

12

Pemigewasset River, North Fork

Difficulty: Class IV/V
Location: Lincoln, NH
River Miles: 12.4 miles (from Zealand Falls),
                    12.3 miles (from below Ethan Pond)
Average Gradient: 100 feet per mile (from Zealand Falls),
                         120 feet per mile (from below Ethan Pond)
USGS Maps: Crawford Notch, South Twin Mt., Mt. Osceola, Lincoln, NH
Portages: 0 (from Zealand Falls), 1 (from below Ethan Pond)

Description:

The North Fork of the Pemigewasset River flows from Ethan Pond and joins the East Branch of the Pemi in the Pemigewasset River Wilderness Area. The run is largely Class III and requires a significant hike to the put-in, but the beauty and remoteness of the Wilderness Area make it worthwhile.

The North Fork can be run in two ways. The first option begins on Whitewall Brook below Zealand Falls and joins the North Fork approximately two miles downstream. Whitewall Brook is a small, meandering stream that drains Zealand Pond below Zealand Hut. The stream contains no good whitewater, and beaver activity sometimes makes the going rough. Several good drops on the North Fork, which lie upstream of the confluence with Whitewall Brook, will be missed using this put-in, but the significantly easier and flatter hike may be worth the sacrifice. Below the confluence, with Whitewall Brook, the North Fork is largely Class II and III with the exception of one Class V drop just above the confluence with the East Branch of the Pemigewasset River. Below this confluence the river becomes much larger and continues Class III and IV, passing under two foot bridges before the take-out at the Route 112 bridge (gage bridge). To make the run longer, continue 2.5 miles to the Loon Mountain Bridge.

The second option is to begin the run on the North Fork itself, below Ethan Pond, the headwaters of the North Fork. From here, the tight riverbed increases in steepness to Thoreau Falls, a steep waterfall, which can be portaged river right. Below the Falls, the river continues over many steep and narrow drops before Whitewall Brook enters on the right. Continue downstream to the take-out as described above.

51

12 PEMIGEWASSET RIVER, NORTH FORK

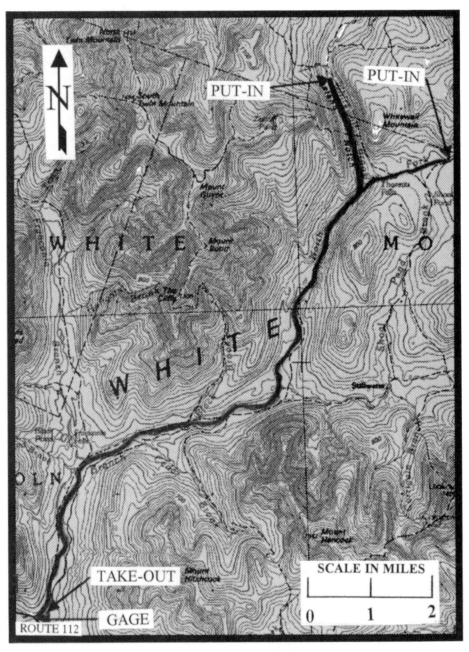

**Reference Maps: USGS, Crawford Notch, NH, 1987; South Twin Mt.,
NH, 1967; Mt. Osceola, NH, 1967; Lincoln, NH, 1967**

Image courtesy of MAPTECH, Inc.

Water Level Information:

There is a gage on the East Branch of the Pemigewasset at the Route 112 bridge (take-out bridge). The gage is painted on the downstream river right side of one of the center bridge piers. It is best seen from the downstream river right side of the bridge. There have not been enough runs on the North Fork to develop a good correlation between this gage and the water levels upstream. However, a level of 1.3 on the bridge gage seems to correlate with a minimum (very low) level on the North Fork.

Two good remote indicators of the level are the Woodstock Gage on the Pemi (Waterline #331173) and the Lincoln Gage on the East Branch of the Pemi (Waterline #335114). Both of these gages are satellite-linked and are available through Waterline and the Internet. A level of 5.7 feet (approximately 2,500 cfs) at the Woodstock Gage seems to correspond to a minimum runnable level.

Shuttle:

The shuttle for the North Fork is the longest of all the runs in this book. To get to the put-in from Interstate 93 north, take Exit 35 to Route 3 north and continue to Route 302 at Twin Mountain. Take a right on Route 302 east and drive approximately 2.5 miles to the sign for Zealand Camping Area. Turn right and continue up the Forest Service road. Go approximately 3.5 miles to a small hiker's lot at the end of this road, which is closed from November through April. From the hiker's lot, hike 2.6 miles to Whitewall Brook below Zealand Falls. Depending on the water level of the Brook, you may need to hike downstream until the stream is large enough to paddle. Put in here.

To get to the put-in below Ethan Pond, from the Zealand Camping Area turn off, continue east on Route 302 past Bretton Woods Ski Area and the Mount Washington Hotel. Continue over Crawford Notch and past the Crawford House to where the Appalachian Trail crosses Route 302. Park here or take a right up a short access road and park at the end of the road. From the end of the road, follow the Appalachian Trail across the railroad tracks, and approximately 2.5 miles to Ethan Pond, the headwaters of the North Fork. Continue past Ethan Pond, with the river on your right, until enough small tributaries enter the river, making the North Fork large enough to paddle. Put in here.

To get to the take-out, follow Route 302 west back to Route 3 south. Take Route 3 to Interstate 93 south through Franconia Notch to Exit 32. Follow Route 112 east past Loon Mountain. Cross the East Branch of the Pemi and park in the Forest Service lot at the Wilderness Trail on the left. This is the normal take-out.

History:

Boyce Greer, Scott Murray, and Greg Hanlon did the first run on the North Fork from below Ethan Pond in the spring of in 1997, in inflatable kayaks. Snowshoes were essential for the hike and a sherpa came in handy for carrying the snowshoes and extra gear back out. The first run from Zealand was done many years before. The exact date of this run and its participants are unknown.

Additional Information:

At the time of this writing, the U.S. Forest Service charges a parking fee for parking in the lot at the take-out bridge. You can pick up a 7-day pass for $5.00 or a seasonal pass (which goes from May 1st to April 30th) for $20.00, at the Visitor Center off Exit 32 in Lincoln, New Hampshire. To avoid this charge, you can paddle an additional two miles and take out at the free parking area at Loon Mountain.

Notes

13

Pemigewasset River ("The Upper Pemi") ***

Difficulty: Class V
Location: Lincoln, NH
River Miles: 2.9 miles
Average Gradient: 200 feet per mile
USGS Maps: Franconia, Lincoln, NH
Portages: 0

Description:

The Upper Pemi, with its vertical waterfalls, numerous slot drops, and consistently runnable water levels, has become a favorite of New England creek boaters. The Upper Pemi flows due south from Profile Lake at the base of Cannon Mountain through Franconia Notch. The normal put-in is just above The Basin, a tourist attraction where one can easily view several interesting waterfalls. From the put-in, the river quickly plunges through narrow slots and over ledges. The best line follows the main flow river left. This drops vertically into a large pothole called The Basin. The river then mellows somewhat until crossing under Interstate 93. About 100 yards beyond the highway, the river plunges through North Pole rapid, which is often portaged, and into the gorge. The Sentinel Pine covered bridge marks a beautiful rapid named Slam Bam which finishes in The Pool. You will pass under one more covered bridge (gage bridge) and run many more rapids and ledge drops before the take-out at the Indian Head Resort on river right.

Water Level Information:

For a New Hampshire creek, the Upper Pemi has very reliable water. The river rises and falls quickly, but can be run at a wide range of flows. The gage is the river left abutment footing platform on the downstream side of the covered bridge below Flume Brook, behind the State Park visitor's center. A level of two inches below the platform is considered a minimum runnable level. A level of two inches above the footing is medium, and one foot above the footing is high. This bridge is sometimes difficult to access when the State Park is charging an admission fee to the Flume area.

55

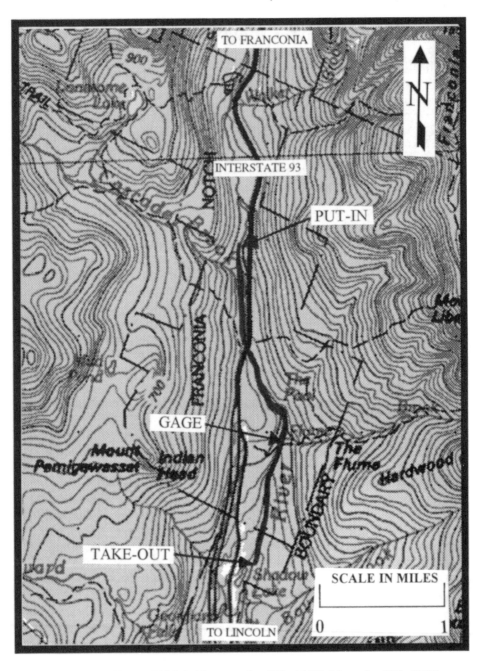

Reference Maps: USGS, Franconia, NH, 1967; Lincoln, NH, 1967

Image courtesy of MAPTECH, Inc.

The Woodstock Gage (Waterline #331173), on the Pemigewasset River below the confluence of the Upper Pemi and the East Branch, also provides an excellent indication of the water level. Flows of 4.5 feet (1,300 cfs), 6.5 feet (3,700 cfs), and 9 feet (9,500 cfs) at Woodstock usually correspond to low, medium, and high levels respectively. The mean monthly flows for April and May at the Woodstock Gage are 1,320 cfs and 1,380 cfs, a low but runnable range (see Appendix). The Woodstock Gage is satellite-linked and is available from Waterline or over the Internet.

Shuttle:

Park in The Basin parking area, accessed from Interstate 93 south in Franconia Notch State Park, and put in on the north side of the lot. From the put-in, take Interstate 93 south to Exit 1. Follow Route 3 south toward Lincoln. The take-out is behind the Indian Head Hotel/Resort on your left. You can usually park in the hotel lot, but please be courteous, as we do not want to lose this privilege. To retrieve a car from the put-in, you need to drive north on Interstate 93 to Exit 2 (Cannon Mountain Tramway exit). Here you can change direction and head south on Interstate 93 back to The Basin exit.

History:

The first known run of the Upper Pemi was on April 26, 1992, by Bob Potter, Gary Weiner, Greg Hanlon, and Steve Hyndman. During this run the boaters put in below The Basin and portaged the North Pole. A complete run, including the North Pole was done several years later.

Additional Information:

The Upper Pemi flows through several unique areas, including The Basin, The Pool, and The Flume. These resources are under careful watch by the State of New Hampshire. We want to continue to paddle this valuable section of river, so please keep a low profile and do not paddle in large groups.

Notes

_____

_____

_____

_____

_____

_____

_____

_____

Wilson River Kern, Upper Pemigewasset River, New Hampshire

14
Sawyer River ***

Difficulty: Class V
Location: Livermore, NH
River Miles: 3.5 miles
Average Gradient: 190 feet per mile
USGS Maps: Bartlett, Mt. Carrigain, NH
Portages: 0

Description:

Sawyer River is one of the best Class V runs in New England. Its consistently steep riverbed, filled with long boulder-choked rapids and interesting ledge drops, make it an excellent first stop when the water is up. The Sawyer is located in the White Mountains of New Hampshire and flows northeast into the Saco River in Crawford Notch. It parallels an old Forest Service road connecting Route 302 to a hiker's parking lot approximately three miles upstream. This road is no longer open to vehicles due to recent erosion. From the put-in at the hiker's parking lot, the river quickly steepens to Class IV, with the rapids increasing in frequency and difficulty.

After about 1.5 miles, the river reaches the abandoned logging settlement of Livermore. Several old building foundations and one complete cabin still remain. This marks the start of House Rapid and the most difficult section of river. The most straightforward line through this drop begins by running the top part of the rapid on the right and then running the left channel below. Beware of the lower right channel, as it can be extremely hazardous, especially at high water. From below House Rapid, the river remains steep and continuous with many distinct rapids. The severity of the rapids slowly tapers as you approach Route 302. Take out river right immediately after the Route 302 bridge but above the railroad bridge. There is a convenient parking area here.

Water Level Information:

Catching the Sawyer at an appropriate water level can be more challenging than the run itself. The river rises and falls very quickly and never seems to stabilize at a good paddling level. You might drive to the Sawyer one day only to find the river too high to run, and yet, by the next morning, the water level can drop significantly, making it too low. This can be frustrating, but when you do finally catch the right level, you won't regret your efforts.

14 SAWYER RIVER ***

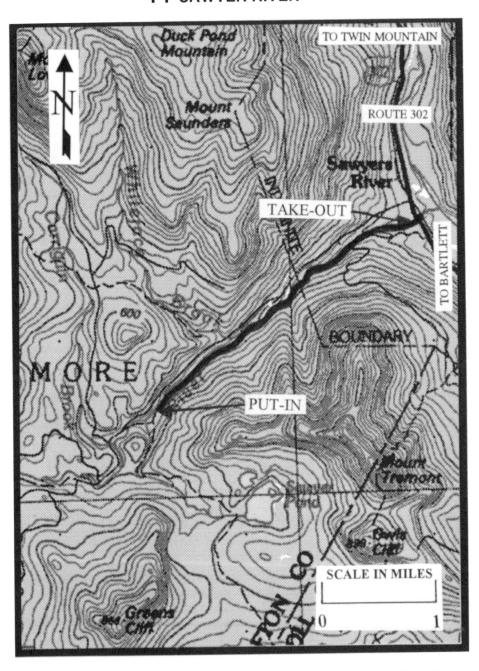

Reference Maps: USGS, Bartlett, NH, 1987; Mt. Carrigain, NH, 1987

Image courtesy of MAPTECH, Inc.

The Sawyer currently has no gage. If it looks bony but runnable at the take-out, it will be fluid upstream. There is a USGS satellite gage on the Saco River near Conway (Waterline #331112) below the confluence of the Sawyer. A correlation has not yet been developed between this gage and the Sawyer. The Woodstock Gage on the Pemigewasset River (Waterline #331173) provides a reasonable indication of the level of the Sawyer, even though it lies in a different watershed. Flows of 5.5 feet (2,300 cfs), 7.5 feet (5,400 cfs), and 8.5 feet (8,000 cfs) at Woodstock usually correspond to low, medium, and high levels respectively. Both the Woodstock Gage and the Conway Gage are satellite-linked and are available from Waterline and the Internet.

Shuttle:

The Sawyer has no shuttle; boaters must walk to the put-in. Park at the lot on the north side of Route 302 next to the highway bridge, which crosses the Sawyer River. Cross Route 302 and continue 3+ miles upstream to the hiker's lot. This is the normal put-in.

History:

The first known run of the Sawyer was April 24, 1992, by Boyce Greer, J.J. Valera, Greg Hanlon, and friends after scouting and removing several trees at low water.

Additional Information:

The Sawyer, like most steep rivers in New Hampshire, tends to collect logs. BEWARE!

Notes

_____

_____

_____

_____

_____

_____

_____

_____

Boyce Greer runs House Rapid, Sawyer River, New Hampshire

Vermont

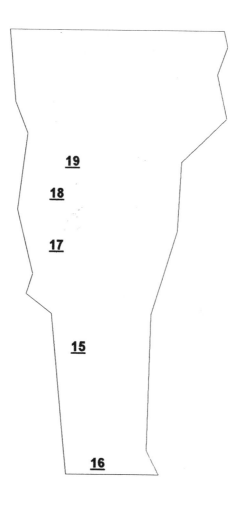

15. Big Branch ***
16. Deerfield River, West Branch ***
17. Middlebury River **
18. New Haven River *
19. Ridley Brook **

15 BIG BRANCH ***

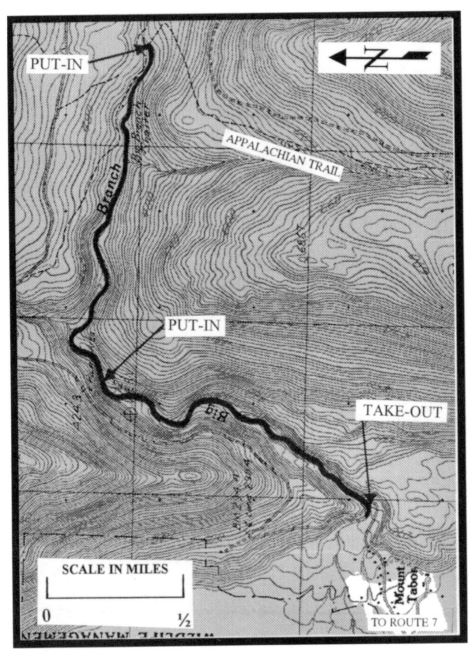

PUT-IN

PUT-IN

TAKE-OUT

APPALACHIAN TRAIL

Branch Big Branch

Big

Mount Tabor

SCALE IN MILES

0   ½

TO ROUTE 7

Reference Map: USGS, Danby, VT, 1986

Image courtesy of MAPTECH, Inc.

15
Big Branch ***

Difficulty: Class V
Location: Mt. Tabor, VT
River Miles: 1.2 miles (from lower put-in)
                  2.6 miles (from upper put-in)
Average Gradient: 260 feet per mile (from lower put-in)
USGS Maps: Danby, VT
Portages: 0

Description:

The Big Branch is definitely a New England gem. It flows southwest from the mountain ridge running from Manchester, Vermont, north toward Rutland. The run is continuous with only small eddies between long, boulder-filled rapids. The river's gradient is moderate above the picnic area put-in and below the take-out. Fortunately, there is a steep gorge section between these two points.

From the picnic area put-in, the drops begin immediately with several unnamed rapids before Spelunk rapid, named for the cave at the bottom of the drop. Shortly below you will pass two old concrete bridge abutments just above Eye Bender. Beware of the twisted I-beams that mark the beginning and end of this rapid. After several more fun rapids lies the biggest drop on the run, BLT (Boof Left Twice). The drops continue to the take-out bridge. The river upstream of the picnic area contains many moderate rapids, which can provide a good warm-up when the water is high.

Water Level Information:

There is no gage on the Big Branch. However, it does hold water very well and it can be run at a wide range of flows. Be careful of judging the flow at the take-out, as the riverbed becomes somewhat narrower and steeper upstream where it is not visible from the road. The Bennington Gage on the Walloomsac River (Waterline #501178) can provide general information about water level trends in the area.

Shuttle:

To get to the Big Branch, follow Route 7 north from Manchester, Vermont, approximately 12 miles to Danby and Mount Tabor. Take a right on Mount Tabor Road toward Mount Tabor. Follow this road one mile to the Big Branch take-out. Park in the pull-off before the bridge. To get to the put-in, continue upstream to the Big Branch picnic area. A switchback trail leads down to the normal put-in. If the water is high, put-in upstream where the Long Trail crosses the river. To get to the high water put-in, continue up the road to the Long Trail. Hike the Long Trail approximately one mile to the river.

History:

The Big Branch was first run by Brian Totten and Steve Heanue in the spring of 1997.

Additional Information:

During the winter, the road along the Big Branch is closed; however, the run is certainly worth the walk from the gate.

Notes

_____

_____

_____

_____

_____

_____

_____

_____

_____

_____

_____

_____

_____

_____

16
Deerfield River, West Branch ***

Difficulty: Class V
Location: Readsboro, VT
River Miles: 3.5 miles
Average Gradient: 155 feet per mile
USGS Map: Readsboro, VT
Portages: 0

Description:

The West Branch of the Deerfield flows southeast through Readsboro, Vermont, where it joins with the main stem of the Deerfield River. From the put-in, the river starts with a bang at Readsboro Falls. Many swims have occurred from the sticky hole at the base of the Falls. If you want to warm up, skip Readsboro Falls and put in below, where the river is generally Class IV until crossing Route 100. Here, the river steepens with Diamond Cutter rapid, 100 yards downstream from the highway bridge. The river then mellows before the most challenging rapid, Tunnel Vision, a long, continuous rapid containing many sharp, angular boulders. You definitely do not want to roll in this rapid. Below Tunnel Vision lies a long, fun stretch of unnamed rapids before you hit two more difficult drops, High Chair and Low Chair. These are run shortly after passing under a footbridge. Continue on the main stem of the Deerfield after the confluence, approximately 0.5 miles to the take-out river right.

Water Level Information:

The gage on the West Branch is a rock located river right just upstream of the bridge on Brooklyn Street between High Chair and Low Chair rapids. A graduated scale is painted on the downstream side of the rock. A level of 0 indicates a minimum runnable level, 5 a medium level, and 8 a high level. All rapids have been run at a level of 10 except Readsboro Falls.

The West Branch rises rapidly but holds water better than many New England creeks. This is probably a result of its sluggish upper watershed, which drains several swampy areas. Although no steadfast correlation has been developed, the satellite gage on the Walloomsac River at Bennington (Waterline #501178), an adjacent drainage, can provide a remote indication of flows in the area of the West Branch. This gage is available via Waterline and over the Internet.

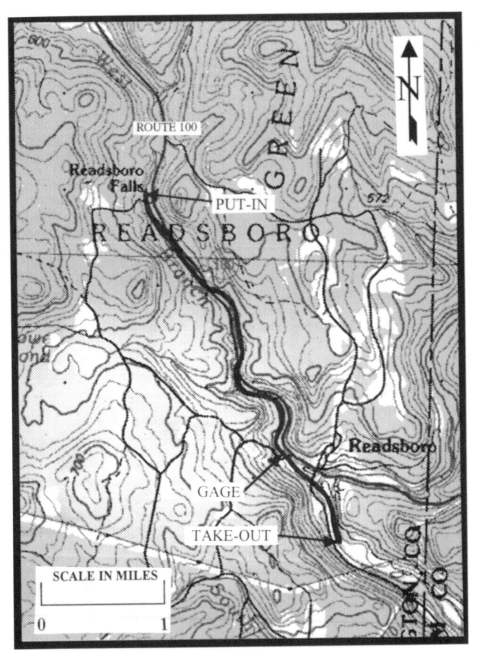

Reference Map: USGS, Readsboro, VT, 1987

Image courtesy of MAPTECH, Inc.

Loosely correlated levels on the Walloomsac of 2 feet (110 cfs), 3 feet (440 cfs), and 4 feet (920 cfs) seem to indicate low, medium, and high levels respectively on the West Branch. If either river is rising or falling sharply, this correlation is inaccurate. The mean monthly flow for April at the Bennington Gage is 540 cfs, a runnable level (see Appendix). The West Branch, like most rivers, is very dangerous at high water levels, so it is best to familiarize yourself with it at lower water.

Shuttle:

Put in on Route 100, just above Readsboro Falls, 2.8 miles upstream from Readsboro, Vermont. A large barn just off the road marks the put-in. To get to the take-out, follow the river downstream to the center of Readsboro. Take a right onto Tunnel Road, going toward Monroe Bridge, Massachusetts. You will cross the West Branch and continue south approximately 0.5 miles past several houses to where the river meets the road. There is a convenient pull-off spot on the left.

History:

Paddlers have been running the West Branch for quite some time due to its roadside location. Its exact history is unknown.

Additional Information:

Boaters beware: the riverbed of Tunnel Vision was altered during the construction of Route 100. The channel is full of sharp boulders. Also, there are difficult rapids within the tunnel itself. You will not be able to scout these rapids. The best line is usually river left.

Notes

_____

_____

_____

_____

_____

_____

_____

John Kern, home free in Tunnel Vision, West Branch of the Deerfield, VT

17
Middlebury River **

Difficulty: Class V
Location: Ripton, VT
River Miles: 2.6 miles
Average Gradient: 200 feet per mile
USGS Map: East Middlebury, VT
Portages: 0

Description:

The Middlebury River flows west from Ripton, Vermont, in the Green Mountain National Forest, to Otter Creek in Middlebury, Vermont. From the put-in, downstream of Ripton, the run begins with several moderate warm-up rapids before the North Branch of the Middlebury enters river right. Shortly below the confluence lies the biggest drop on the run. This fairly long rapid, which is run river right, ends with a vertical drop into a deep pool. Below this drop, several rapids lead to the Birth Canal, The Catcher's Mitt, and Afterbirth. Many more rapids, including Tester and Your Mom, lead to the take-out at the first bridge over the river. Take out river right.

Water Level Information:

There is no gage on the Middlebury River; however, it can be run at a wide range of flows. Be careful of judging the flows at either the put-in or the take-out. The riverbed narrows and steepens near the middle of the run where it is not visible from the road. The Middlebury Gage on the New Haven River (Waterline # 501158) can provide general information about water level trends in the area. Levels of 3.8 feet (195 cfs) and 4.5 feet (400 cfs) seem to correspond respectively with low and medium levels on the Middlebury. This gage is available via Waterline over the Internet.

Shuttle:

To get to the put-in, drive west on Route 125 from Ripton, Vermont toward Middlebury. The put-in is west of Ripton and just downstream of where Route 125 crosses the Middlebury River. To get to the take-out, drive approximately 2.5 miles west on Route 125 toward Middlebury to the first bridge across the river. This is the take-out bridge.

17 MIDDLEBURY RIVER **

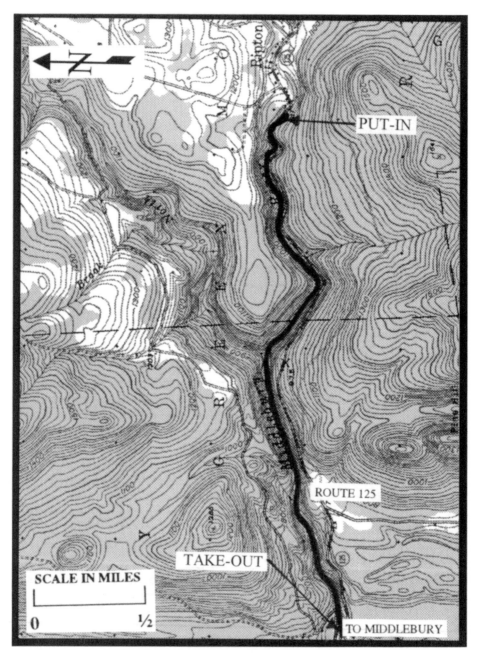

Reference Map: USGS, East Middlebury, VT, 1983

Image courtesy of MAPTECH, Inc.

History:

The Middlebury was first run by the Kern brothers and friends in the fall of 1994. Prior runs were attempted, but the difficult gorge was portaged.

Additional Information:

The Catcher's Mitt is a recirculating eddy with overhanging walls. It is very difficult to swim out of this eddy. If you flip while entering The Mitt, be sure you do not come out of your boat. If you swim, it will surely be an unpleasant experience. Due to its steep and narrow characteristics, the Middlebury has a reputation for acquiring new strainers regularly. Be careful.

Notes

18 NEW HAVEN RIVER *

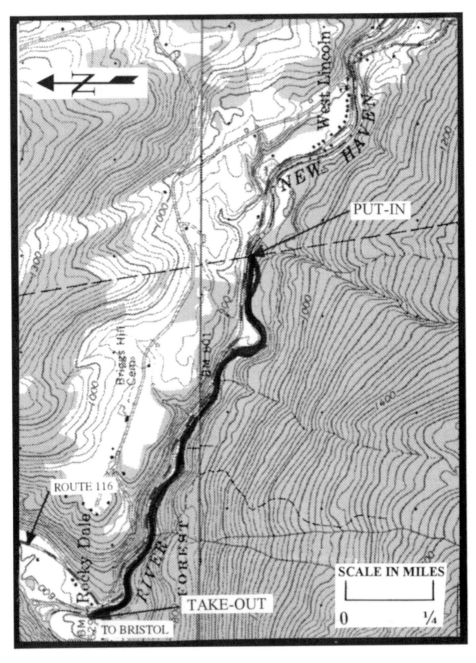

Reference Maps: USGS, South Mt., VT, 1963; Bristol, VT, 1963

Image courtesy of MAPTECH, Inc.

18

New Haven River *

Difficulty: Class V
Location: Bristol, VT
River Miles: 1.3 miles
Average Gradient: 165 feet per mile
USGS Map: South Mt., Bristol, VT
Portages: 0

Description:

The New Haven River, which runs west through Bristol, Vermont, is one of the more popular steep creeks in the state. The riverbed consists mainly of boulder-filled rapids and good ledge drops. From the put-in, the run begins slowly with several tricky boulder gardens before Lost Legs rapid, which contains two river-wide ledges with holes that can be sticky at some levels. The next significant rapid is Toaster Falls, which can be downright intimidating. This is the hardest drop on the river. The drop is usually run river left by sliding down the sloping entrance ramp and then dropping off the 15+ foot vertical fall. The drop is named Toaster Falls because of the narrow deep spot at the base of the falls. If you run too far left or right, a solid piton is likely. Toaster has been run in the center and far river right, but these lines are not recommended for the lighthearted. Several more good drops, including Squared Off and Mama Tried, lie between Toaster and the take-out, which is just below the highway bridge river left.

Water Level Information:

The New Haven holds water very well for a run of its steepness, and can also be run at a wide range of water levels. Paddlers use a large flat rock as the gage, and this is located river right, just downstream of the take-out bridge. If the water is just at the top of the rock, the flow is medium; if the water is over the rock, the level is high. Also, most of the river is visible from the road, so it is easy to make a roadside level check. A satellite link has recently been added to gage on the New Haven River near Middlebury (Waterline # 501158). Since this is a recent addition to the network, a reliable correlation between this gage and boatable levels on the New Haven has not yet been developed. However, water levels of 4.5 feet (400 cfs) and 6.5 feet (1,480 cfs) seem to correspond to medium and high levels, respectively.

Shuttle:

To get to the put-in from Bristol, Vermont, take Route 116 west toward Rocky Dale. Just after crossing the New Haven in Rocky Dale, take a right on Lincoln Road and follow along the river right bank toward West Lincoln. Put in approximately 1.5 miles up this road, above all visible rapids, before entering West Lincoln. To get to the take-out, drive downstream toward Rocky Dale. The take-out is at the Route 116 bridge over the New Haven.

History: Unknown.

Additional Information:

If the water is very low and you have already made the trip, it can be fun to do a bone run from Toaster Falls down. The floods in the summer of 1998 changed the river significantly, making many rapids more fluid.

Notes

_____

_____

_____

_____

_____

_____

_____

_____

_____

_____

_____

_____

_____

_____

_____

19
Ridley Brook **

Difficulty: Class V
Location: Duxbury, VT
River Miles: 1.4 miles (from lower put-in)
Average Gradient: 250 feet per mile
USGS Map: Waterbury, VT
Portages: 0

Description:

Ridley Brook flows north from Camel's Hump State Park, just south of North Duxbury, Vermont, into the Winooski River. This run is continuous, steep and tight, with easy roadside access from Camel's Hump Road. Once you are familiar with the run, it can be done quickly. This can make for a nice multi-river day when combined with the Middlebury, the New Haven, or both.

The rapids consist of steep boulder gardens, ledge drops, and tight chutes. From the put-in, the action starts immediately with several moderate drops before the river crosses under Camel's Hump Road. From here the river is pool drop but continuous. The more significant drops include Bathtub, Back Yard Boating, and Video Drop. The intensity of the run diminishes shortly above the take-out. Take out at the second bridge crossing the river. With good boat-scouting skills, many of the rapids can be seen from the river; however, some scouting is necessary for those not familiar with the run. Beware of judging the difficulty of the run from the road, as the more difficult rapids will not be visible.

Water Level Information:

There is no gage on Ridley Brook, but the river can easily be seen from several points along Camel's Hump Road. Due to its steep and small drainage area, the water level of Ridley Brook rises and falls very quickly and can therefore be difficult to catch at a runnable level. Although Ridley can be run at a wide range of flows, as always, beware of high water if you are unfamiliar with the run. There is currently no reliable remote indicator of the level of Ridley Brook. The Middlebury Gage on the New Haven River (Waterline # 501158) can provide general information about water level trends in the area. This gage is available via Waterline and over the Internet.

19 RIDLEY BROOK **

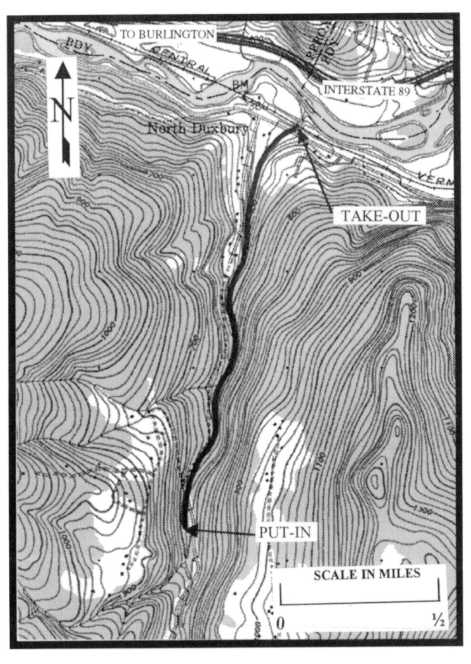

Reference Map: USGS, Waterbury, VT, 1980

Image courtesy of MAPTECH, Inc.

Shuttle:

From Montpelier, follow Route 89 north to Exit 9 in Middlesex, Vermont. Take Route 2 west, toward Waterbury, crossing the Winooski River. Take a left on Route 100 south and a quick right on River Road. Follow River Road along the south bank of the Winooski River. Just after crossing Ridley Brook in North Duxbury, take a left on Camel's Hump Road to your desired put-in. The normal put-in is between the first and second bridges on Camel's Hump Road crossing Ridley Brook; however, when the water is high, some paddlers put in further upstream past the second bridge and take out at the normal put-in.

History:

Ridley Brook was first run by John Guerriere, Willy Kern, and Chuck Kern in 1994. Since then, many paddlers have enjoyed this Vermont steep creek treasure.

Additional Information:

Since Ridley Brook and Preston Brook are similar and have adjacent drainage areas, there has been much confusion between these runs. When Ridley was first run, the paddlers believed they had run Preston Brook, and therefore called Ridley Brook "Preston Brook" for quite some time. This confusion still exists with much of the boating community. At high water levels, it is fun to paddle into the Winooski River and take out below Railroad Tressel rapid.

Notes

_____

_____

_____

_____

_____

_____

_____

_____

_____

_____

Boyce Greer running Amuck, Gulf Hagas, Maine

Maine

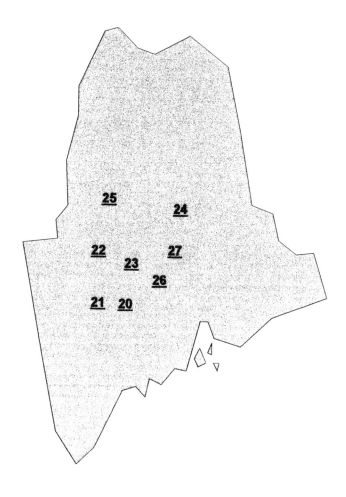

20. Austin Stream
21. Carrying Place Stream
22. Cold Stream
23. Moxie Stream *
24. Nesowadnehunk Stream **
25. Penobscot River, South Branch
26. Piscataquis River, East Branch *
27. Pleasant River, West Branch ("Gulf Hagas") ***

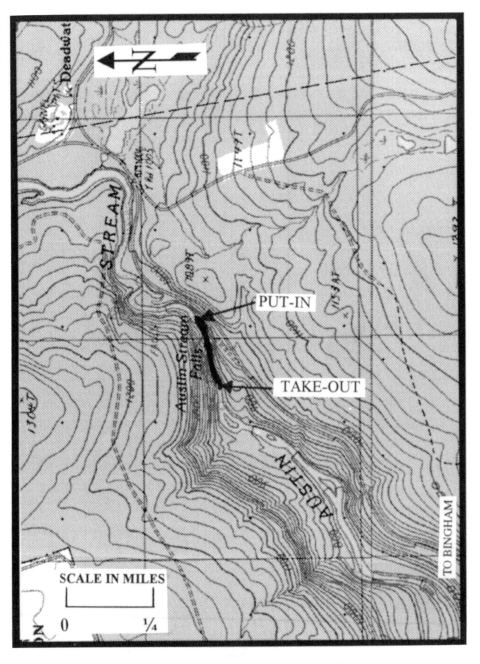

PUT-IN

TAKE-OUT

SCALE IN MILES

0   ¼

Reference Map: USGS, Dimmick Mt., ME, 1989

Image courtesy of MAPTECH, Inc.

20
Austin Stream

Difficulty: Class V
Location: Moscow, ME
River Miles: 0.2 miles
Average Gradient: 390 feet per mile
USGS Map: Dimmick Mt., ME
Portages: 1

Description:

Austin Stream possesses a very short but beautiful series of drops called Austin Falls. The Stream flows south into the Kennebec River in Bingham, Maine. Although it would be difficult to occupy an entire day at Austin Stream, it can make for an interesting afternoon following a morning run on the Kennebec. Put in above the Falls next to the logging road and run a series of sloping and vertical ledge drops which cut through a deep bedrock gorge. The last vertical drop is usually portaged, except at high water levels when you can run left, avoiding the rocks in the shallow landing pool. Take out river left in the pool below this fall and climb up a steep hill back to the dirt road.

Water Level Information:

There is no gage on Austin Stream; however, it is easy to see the entire run to determine if the level is suitable. The river is usually run at low to medium-low levels. Both above and below the Falls, the riverbed is much wider. Within the Falls section, the river is more constricted and therefore requires little water to run. If other area creeks (such as Cold Stream) are at good levels, Austin Stream is probably very high. Don't be discouraged if Austin Stream looks exceptionally low where it crosses Route 201 in Bingham. The run lies in a far more constricted stretch of river.

Shuttle:

To get to Austin Stream from Bingham, Maine, drive north on Route 201. At the edge of town, take a right on Route 16, just before crossing Austin Stream. Continue upstream along the river left bank approximately 0.8 miles and take a left onto a dirt road that rises away from the river. Follow this road for 5.8 miles to Austin Falls. Park in the pull off on the left. No shuttle is necessary, as the run is very short.

History:

The first known run of Austin Stream was in the summer of 1992 by Boyce Greer and Greg Hanlon. During this run, the final waterfall was portaged. This final drop has since been run.

Notes

_____

_____

_____

_____

_____

_____

_____

_____

_____

_____

_____

_____

_____

_____

_____

_____

_____

_____

_____

_____

_____

_____

21

Carrying Place Stream

Difficulty: Class V
Location: Carrying Place Township, ME
River Miles: 2.3 miles
Average Gradient: 145 feet per mile
USGS Maps: East Carry Pond, Caratunk, ME
Portages: 0

Description:

Carrying Place Stream drains from East Carry Pond into Wyman Lake on the Kennebec River. Like many runs in the area, most of the rapids are formed by carved bedrock; however, there are some boulder-filled drops and, at low levels, some shallow bony rapids. From the put-in, the river quickly becomes technical with several good drops and then an interesting slide drop. The next significant rapid, which is approximately half way through the run, is the biggest rapid. The drop consists of a large (30-foot) cascade landing in shallow water. Although you can paddle this rapid in a hard boat, it may be more fun in a duck. Scout or portage river right. Take out river right in a small sandpit where the stream enters the lake.

Water Level Information:

There is no gage on Carrying Place Stream; however, it runs frequently in the spring and after heavy rainfall. Its flow can be checked at the last rapid where the stream enters Wyman Lake. This drop is usually fairly bony, so if there is enough water here, it should be high enough upstream. With a sharp eye or a pair of binoculars, it is also possible to check the flow from Route 201 across Wyman Lake where Carrying Place Stream enters the Lake. This may save a long drive only to discover the river has no water. There is currently no reliable remote indicator of the level of Carrying Place Stream. However, the Blanchard Gage on the Piscataquis River (Waterline # 235113) can provide general information about water level trends in the area. This gage is available via Waterline and over the Internet.

21 CARRYING PLACE STREAM

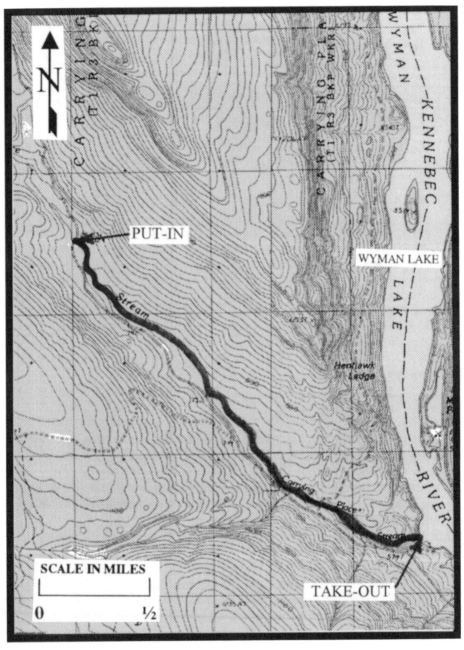

**Reference Maps: USGS, East Carrying Pond, ME 1989;
Caratunk, ME, 1989**
Image courtesy of MAPTECH, Inc.

Shuttle:

From Skowhegan, Maine, take Route 201 north to Bingham and turn left on Route 16 west. Just after crossing the Kennebec River, take your first right. Continue along the river right bank of the Kennebec to Wyman Lake. The road turns west away from the lake. Take your first right, just after crossing Houston Brook, upstream of Houston Falls, and follow along the west shore of the lake. As the road turns away from the lake, it follows the river right bank of Carrying Place Stream. Put in at the first bridge across the main stream. To get to the take-out, follow the logging road back to a sandpit where the stream enters the lake.

History:

Carrying Place Stream was first run sometime in the early 1990s.

Notes

22 COLD STREAM

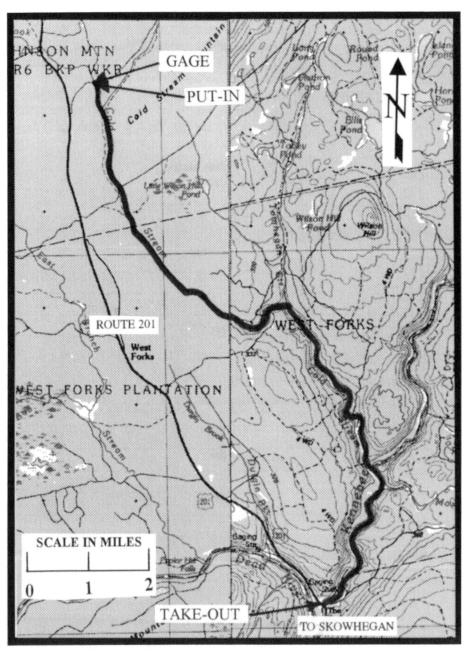

Reference Maps: USGS, Johnson Mt., ME, 1989; Black Brook Pond, ME, 1988; The Forks, ME, 1988

Image courtesy of MAPTECH, Inc.

22
Cold Stream

Difficulty: Class V
Location: Johnson Mountain Township, ME
River Miles: 8.5 miles (on Cold Stream)
               3 miles (on the Kennebec River)
Average Gradient: 65 feet per mile (on Cold Stream)
USGS Maps: Johnson Mt., Black Brook Pond, The Forks, ME
Portages: 0

Description:

Do not be deceived by the relatively low average gradient of only 65 feet per mile of Cold Stream. At appropriate water levels, Cold Stream can be a fun creek with several good drops separated by quick water and easy rapids. From the put-in, the rapids build in difficulty. The river drops over many bedrock ledges, narrow slots, and vertical falls. The most significant rapid on the run is the Gorge drop, which is steep and narrow, ending in a near vertical waterfall into shallow water. Most of the significant drops on Cold Stream are steep ledge drops formed by exposed bedrock. The run mellows considerably toward the confluence of Cold Stream and the Kennebec River.

Water Level Information:

Cold Stream usually runs much of the spring and after any significant rainfall. This stream is even run in midsummer. There is no remote indicator of the level of Cold Stream; however, there is a graduated metal staff gage on the downstream river left abutment of the put-in bridge. This gage was moved when the bridge was rebuilt a couple of years ago, making old reference stages invalid. Boaters also use the large, flat rock in the center of the stream, just downstream of the put-in bridge, to gage the water level. If the top surface of this rock is partially covered, the water is at a minimum runnable level. If the rock is just fully covered, the level is good. If the rock is buried, the level is high. The Blanchard Gage on the Piscataquis River (Waterline # 235113) can provide general information about water level trends in the area. This gage is available via Waterline and over the Internet.

Shuttle:

To get to the put-in from The Forks, Maine, take Route 201 north 7.8 miles to a dirt logging road on the right. Take this road and continue past a logging equipment storage facility on your left. Go approximately one mile from Route 201 to a small one-lane bridge (gage bridge) over Cold Stream. Put in here. To get to the take-out, drive back to Route 201, take a left and continue back to The Forks. The take-out is where Route 201 crosses the Kennebec River in The Forks. Park on either side of the bridge.

History: Unknown.

Additional Information:

There is at least one old logging road that accesses Cold Stream between the put-in and the take-out. This provides reasonable access to Route 201 in case a problem arises. Approximately 2.5 miles upstream of the normal put-in lies another series of drops called Cold Stream Falls. This section is not normally paddled, but is accessible via a rugged logging road/trail that roughly follows the stream on river left.

Notes

_____

_____

_____

_____

_____

_____

_____

_____

_____

_____

_____

_____

_____

_____

23
Moxie Stream *

Difficulty: Class V
Location: Moxie Gore, ME
River Miles: 1.8 miles
Average Gradient: 125 feet per mile
USGS Map: The Forks, ME
Portages: 0

Description:

Moxie Stream flows from Moxie Pond in West Forks, Maine, into the Kennebec River. The run is short with the best stretch of whitewater just above Moxie Falls, a beautiful 80-foot vertical waterfall easily visible from wooden platforms constructed for visitors. From the put-in at a washed out snowmobile bridge, the river starts slowly with a couple of easy rapids and some flatwater. After paddling these Class III rapids, you will come to the hardest drop on the run, Junior Falls, a large slide usually run hard left. Several moderate rapids follow, including Slip and Slide, before approaching the final series of ledge drops directly above Moxie Falls and the take-out. The start of this series of drops is marked with a 20-foot sloping slide called The Slide, with two distinct routes followed by The Mushroom Drop, The Shelf, and Double Hammer.

Following the ledge drops, the river turns slightly right, then left immediately over Moxie Falls. *Paddlers must be very aware of this take-out, as Moxie Falls comes up quickly.* One paddler who wasn't aware had to swim Double Hammer, and was fortunate enough to retrieve his boat from below the Falls. Take out river left above the Falls and climb to the access stairs and viewing platform.

Water Level Information:

The water level of Moxie Stream is controlled almost entirely by the Moxie Pond Dam located upstream of the put-in. Although Moxie can be run at a wide range of flows, the stream rarely gets very high due to the dam. Unfortunately, the boater's gage located on the snowmobile bridge at the put-in was washed away some years ago. The best way to gage the flow is to look at the series of drops at the take-out. If these look runnable, the rest of the run is probably okay.

23 MOXIE STREAM *

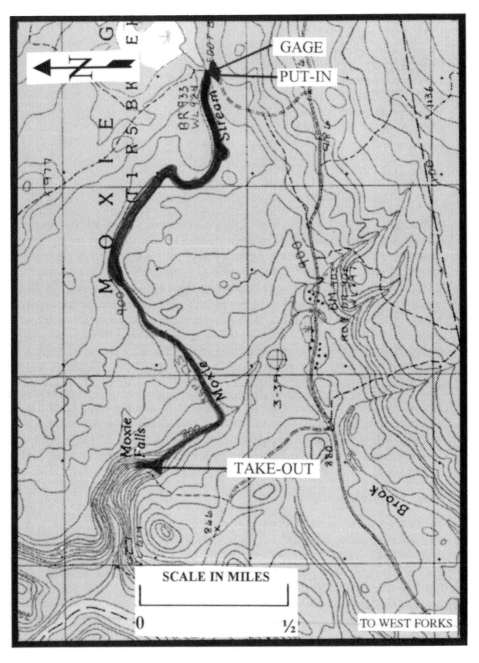

Reference Map: USGS, The Forks, ME, 1988

Image courtesy of MAPTECH, Inc.

You can also drive to the Moxie Pond Dam to check the flow. If the ledge drop directly below the dam looks good, the run is probably okay. Moxie usually runs most of the spring months through May. It runs again in late October or early November, when Kennebec Water and Power Company draws down Moxie Pond to free up storage for high spring flows.

Shuttle:

To reach the Moxie Stream put-in from Berry's General Store in The Forks, Maine, drive south on Route 201 for 200 yards and cross the Kennebec River. Take your first left and travel 3.3 miles to a small dirt road on the left. Turn left and follow this dirt road until you come to a clearing on the left. Park here and carry your boat down the road 0.2 miles to a washed-out snowmobile bridge that crosses Moxie Stream. To reach the take-out from the clearing, go back to the paved road and turn right. Drive 1.2 miles to a better dirt road on the right. This road lies directly before the Moxie Trailhead parking area. Follow this road until the Moxie Falls trail crosses the road and park here. The hiking trail on the right leads to the take-out, which is approximately 0.3 miles.

History:

Although many paddlers made earlier runs on Moxie Stream, the first complete run from the snowmobile bridge to above Moxie Falls, including Junior Falls, was made in 1992 by Greg Hanlon.

Additional Information:

Knowing the location of the take-out is critical for preventing an inadvertent first descent of the 80-foot Moxie Falls. It would be prudent to go to the take-out first so you will recognize it from the river. Also, the parking area at the take-out is very small (typically fits 3 vehicles). If it is full, you can park at the Moxie Falls trailhead on the main road and carry your boat out on the trail.

Notes

_____

_____

_____

_____

_____

_____

_____

_____

Wilson River Kern enters Junior Falls, Moxie Stream, Maine

24
Nesowadnehunk Stream **

Difficulty: Class V
Location: Baxter State Park, ME
River Miles: 3.0 miles (on Nesowadnehunk Stream)
Average Gradient: 155 feet per mile (on Nesowadnehunk Stream)
USGS Map: Rainbow Lake East, ME
Portages: 0

Description:

Nesowadnehunk Stream flows south from Nesowadnehunk Pond through Baxter State Park. It joins the West Branch of the Penobscot River between the Nesowadnehunk Deadwater and the Abol Deadwater just downstream of Nesowadnehunk Falls. The beauty of this run is astonishing. Many of the drops are formed by the pink granite bedrock, which makes up much of the riverbed. Put in at an old dam site within Baxter State Park. The action starts quickly with Little Niagara Falls followed by Big Niagara Falls, an extremely serious drop which has been run by very few people. Many more rapids and ledge drops lie downstream, including Windy Pitch and Indian Pitch, before reaching the confluence with the Penobscot. Take out river right approximately 0.5 miles beneath the confluence where the Penobscot River meets the logging road (the Golden Road).

Water Level Information:

The flow of Nesowadnehunk Stream is controlled by the dam at Nesowadnehunk Pond, which is owned by Great Northern Paper Company. There is no gage on Nesowadnehunk Stream. The best way to judge the level is to look at Nesowadnehunk at the confluence of the Penobscot River. At the confluence, Nesowadnehunk Stream flows over a series of steep ledges. If there appears to be good flow over these drops across the majority of the riverbed, the level is probably okay. There is a small, private cabin with a gated driveway directly across the Penobscot from the Nesowadnehunk confluence. The ledges are visible from here. Nesowadnehunk flow information is sometimes available by calling the Great Northern Paper Company flow line (207-723-2328).

24 NESOWADNEHUNK STREAM **

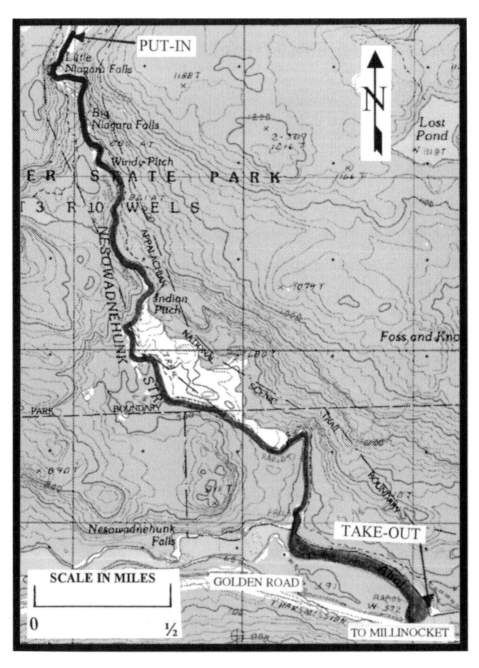

Reference Map: USGS, Rainbow Lake East, ME, 1988
Image courtesy of MAPTECH, Inc.

Shuttle:

From Millinocket, Maine, drive northwest toward Baxter State Park. The Nesowadnehunk Stream runs most often in the spring, when the roads into Baxter State Park are closed. This necessitates carrying your boat upstream from the confluence with the West Branch of the Penobscot River, which lies outside the Park. Bowater Company owns the road along the West Branch of the Penobscot (the Golden Road) and charges an access fee to enter this area. Park in the pull-off at Nesowadnehunk Falls and put in on the West Branch of the Penobscot. Paddle down to the confluence of Nesowadnehunk Stream. The Appalachian Trail follows Nesowadnehunk Stream on river left for the entire length of the run. Hike upriver on the Appalachian Trail approximately 2.5 miles to an old dam site above Little Niagara Falls. Put in here.

To get to the take-out, drive downstream from Nesowadnehunk Falls until the logging road joins the West Branch of the Penobscot at the Abol Deadwater. This is a convenient take-out. If the park roads are open, enter the park at the Togue Pond gate (south entrance) and bear left at the first fork. Follow this road past Tracy Pond. Take a left toward the Daicey Pond Campground. Put in along this road.

History:

The first complete descent of Nesowadnehunk Stream, with no portages, was done by Shannon Carroll, B. J. Johnson, and Brent Toepper in May of 1998.

Notes

_____

_____

_____

_____

_____

_____

_____

_____

_____

25 PENOBSCOT RIVER, SOUTH BRANCH

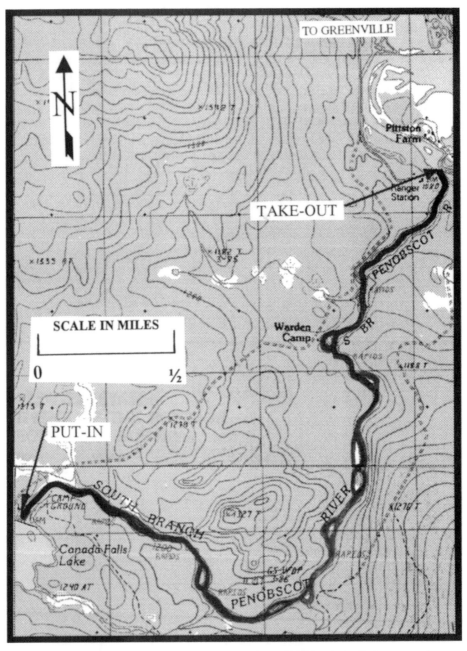

Reference Maps: USGS, Tomhegan Pond, ME, 1989; Seboomook Lake West, ME, 1989
Image courtesy of MAPTECH, Inc.

25
Penobscot River, South Branch

Difficulty: Class V
Location: Pittston Academy Grant, ME
River Miles: 3.5 miles
Average Gradient: 45 feet per mile
USGS Maps: Tomhegan Pond, Seboomook Lake West, ME
Portages: 0

Description:

The South Branch of the Penobscot River flows easterly from Canada Falls Lake into Seboomook Lake, where the North Branch and the South Branch form the West Branch of the Penobscot. The South Branch is one of the easier runs described in this book. It has a very reliable flow and easily accessible water level information, making it an excellent run for paddlers beginning to paddle Class V creeks.

From the put-in below the dam at Canada Falls Lake, the river is generally pool drop. Most of the rapids are formed by bedrock ledges, typical of many Maine creeks. The rapids build in difficulty to where the river splits around a small island, which marks the biggest drop on the run. Here, the river narrows and funnels over a steep slide, which can be scouted or portaged river right. Below lies several more interesting drops before the river calms above the take-out. Take out at the first bridge over the river.

Water Level Information:

Since the put-in to the run lies just downstream of Canada Falls Dam, the entire flow is regulated, making the river sometimes runnable when other area creeks are too low. Also, the river may not rise with rainfall as expected. Water level information is available by calling the Great Northern Paper Company flow line (207-723-2328). Flows of 400 cfs, 900 cfs, and 3,000 cfs correspond to low, medium, and high levels respectively. Great Northern draws down Canada Falls Lake during late August and September, usually providing good medium flows.

Shuttle:

A detailed map of the area, such as a DeLorme Maine Atlas and Gazetteer, will be helpful in finding this fairly out-of-the-way run. It may also help you to avoid getting lost in the maze of logging roads in the area. From Greenville, Maine, follow Lily Bay Road along the east side of Moosehead Lake past Kokadjo to Greenville Road. Take a left (west) on the Golden Road, a toll road, and continue past Caribou Lake and Seboomook Lake. After Seboomook Lake, take a left crossing the North Branch of the Penobscot. Continue to a second left, then a right toward Canada Falls Lake Dam and campground. Put in here. To get to the take-out, drive back the way you came to the first intersection and then take a right. You will soon cross the South Branch, where you will see the take-out bridge by Pittston Farm.

History: Unknown.

Additional Information:

The West Branch of the Penobscot River below Seboomook Lake, known as the Seboomook run, is a good nearby play run and a perfect warm-up for the South Branch. Seboomook flows are also available from the flow phone. Above 900 cfs is adequate. Also, there is good, hearty food available at the restaurant at Pittston Farm, near the take out of the South Branch.

Notes

_____

_____

_____

_____

_____

_____

_____

_____

_____

_____

_____

_____

Bill Dalham, East Branch of the Piscataquis River, Maine

26 PISCATAQUIS RIVER, EAST BRANCH ("EAST PIS") *

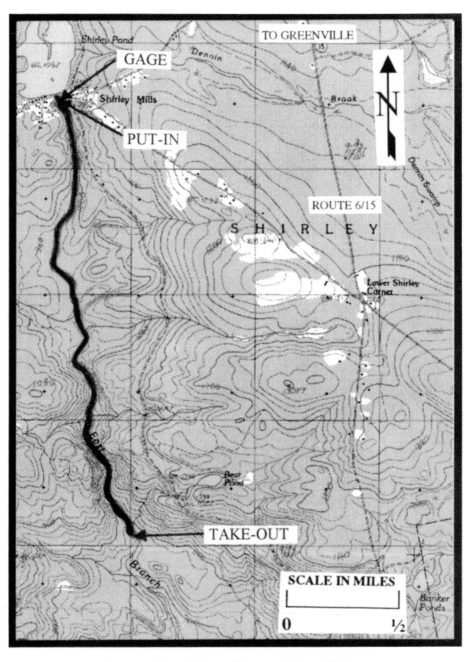

Reference Map: USGS, Monson West, ME, 1989
Image courtesy of MAPTECH, Inc.

26

Piscataquis River, East Branch ("East Pis") *

Difficulty: Class V
Location: Shirley Mills, ME
River Miles: 2.5 miles (to upper take-out)
                    3.8 miles (to lower take-out)
Average Gradient: 105 feet per mile (to upper take-out)
USGS Map: Monson West, ME
Portages: 0

Description:

The East Branch of the Piscataquis River flows due south from Shirley Pond, in the town of Shirley Mills, Maine. Put in at the dam, which impounds Shirley Pond. The drops begin approximately 50 yards downstream from the dam. The first few rapids consist of vertical ledge drops. The river continues through several flat stretches separated by abrupt ledges. The three best drops on the river then follow in close succession. First the river plunges right, into a narrow slot. This is followed by a steep 25-foot ledge drop, which leads into an intimidating series of cascades with some chunky ledges midstream. At low flows it is best to take out here, as the remainder of the run is remarkably bony. At higher flows, continue downstream another 1.3 miles to the lower take-out.

Water Level Information:

The water level of the East Branch of the Piscataquis is sometimes difficult to judge. The best indicator is the weir dam at the put-in. The water entering the riverbed flows from the lake over the top of the dam. A level of 3 inches of flow over the dam indicates a minimum runnable level, whereas a level of 6 inches of flow over the dam indicates a medium level. Don't worry if the drop immediately below the dam looks bony; it will look this way even at high levels. There is a satellite-linked gage on the Piscataquis at Blanchard (Waterline # 235113); however, no steadfast correlation for this gage and the level of the East Pis has been developed. The Blanchard Gage includes flows of both the East and West branches of the Piscataquis and is available via Waterline and over the Internet. Although not a perfect correlation, water levels of 6 feet (640 cfs) and 7 feet (1,320 cfs) at the Blanchard Gage usually indicate high levels on East Branch.

Shuttle:

To get to the put-in from Greenville, Maine, drive south on Route 6-15 approximately 6 miles to Upper Shirley Corner. Take a right on Shirley Mills Road and continue 1.4 miles to Shirley Pond. The Pond is on the right and the dam on the left. Put in below the dam on river left. To get to the take-out, drive back toward Route 6-15. Drive approximately 50 yards from the dam and take your first right onto an old railroad bed-logging road. Drive approximately 2.3 miles to a small stream crossing under the road and a cabin on the left. The low water take-out is where this stream meets the East Branch. To get to the high water take-out, continue on this logging road and take a right down a steep, washed-out logging road. Park in the clearing where a small trail leads to the river. Take out here.

History:

The first complete run of all drops on the East Pis was made in 1992 by Scott Murray, Greg Hanlon, and friends. Earlier, partial runs were also made.

Additional Information:

Although the shuttle road appears firm, it can be very muddy. This is particularly true in the spring. If you are not careful, a boating day can quickly turn into a vehicle extraction day. Towing assistance for flatlanders can and has been obtained for reasonable rates from the loggers in Shirley Mills. The lower take-out is difficult to find from the river. It might be helpful to go here first so you will recognize it from the river.

Notes

_____

_____

_____

_____

_____

_____

_____

_____

_____

27

Pleasant River, West Branch ("Gulf Hagas") ***

Difficulty: Class V
Location: Bowdoin College Grant East, ME
River Miles: 4.7 miles
Average Gradient: 110 feet per mile
USGS Maps: Hay Mt., Barren Mt. East, ME
Portages: 0

Description:

It is with good reason that the West Branch of the Pleasant, or "Gulf Hagas" as it is commonly called, is the most popular Class V creek in Maine. The run contains a unique mix of steep, boulder-choked rapids, ledge drops, and vertical waterfalls. The riverbed descends from a flat, swampy area through the majestic Gulf Hagas Gorge. Vertical and overhanging granite walls line the river throughout the run, making the scenery alone worth the trip. Regrettably, you may be too preoccupied to enjoy the scenery around you, especially if it is your first run.

From the put-in bridge (gage bridge), the river winds through a flat, marshy area until the river splits. Follow the widest channel, which cascades left and leads to the first rapid, Stairs Falls. Immediately after the first rapid, the river rejoins the right flow channel and goes over two small ledge drops. Shortly below these lies a 12+ foot vertical waterfall called Faceplant, just above the classic, 18-foot Billings Falls. The overhanging granite walls that close in above can help you to identify the next major rapid, the most difficult on the run. This drop, appropriately named Amuck (because here you may not want to run amuck), is scoutable on river right and often portaged.

Below Amuck, and still within the Gorge, the river continues over many drops, including Buttermilk Falls, Jaws, and the Hammond Street Pitch, before its walls open. Take out where the Appalachian Trail crosses the river at a wide, shallow area called the Hermitage. A trail sign is visible on river right. Follow the trail 100 yards to the parking area on the logging road.

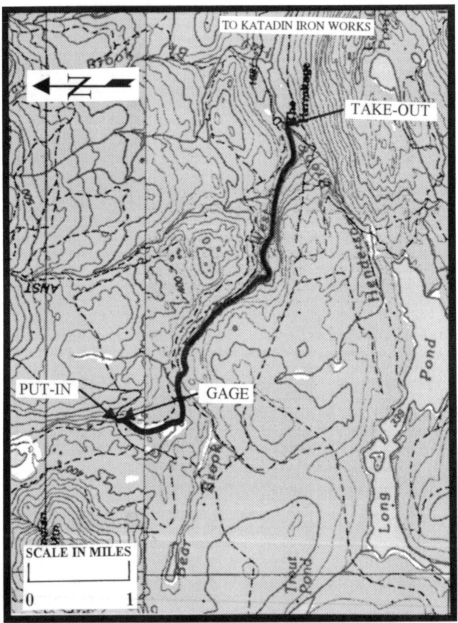

Reference Maps: USGS, Hay Mt., ME, 1988; Barren Mt. East, ME, 1988

Image courtesy of MAPTECH, Inc.

Water Level Information:

The Gulf Hagas is usually runnable in the late spring or after any heavy rainfall. The gage used to judge the water level is the downstream, river right abutment footing of the put-in bridge. A level of 4 inches below the footing indicates a minimum runnable level, a level even with the abutment indicates a medium level, and a level 8 inches above the footing indicates a high level. Although there is no really accurate way of judging the water level of the Pleasant remotely, it is possible to use the satellite-linked gage on the Piscataquis River at Blanchard (Waterline # 235113) to approximate the level of the Pleasant. If the Piscataquis is high, or rising, the same is likely true for the Pleasant. A water level of 7 feet (1,320 cfs) or above usually corresponds to high water on the Pleasant. This gage is available via Waterline and over the Internet.

Shuttle:

To get to the take-out from Brownville Junction, Maine, follow Route 11 north approximately 5 miles. Take a left at a sign for Katahdin Ironworks onto a paved road which quickly turns to dirt. Follow this road approximately 6 miles to a rope gate at the remains of the Katahdin Ironworks. The Gulf Hagas, although on public land, is only accessible by private roads managed by Katahdin Iron Works/Mary-Jo Inc., who charge a toll to use their usually dilapidated dirt roads. At the time of this writing, the current toll is $4.00 per person for Maine residents and $7.00 per person for out-of-state residents. Pay the toll at the gate and continue 6.5 miles to the dirt parking area (take-out) on the right where a short trail leads down to the river. To get to the put-in, continue up the same road for 5.5 miles. The road will bend slightly to the right before crossing the river at a small, one lane bridge (gage bridge). Put in here.

To get to the take-out from Main Street in Greenville Center, take a right on Pleasant Street, which turns into East Road before passing the airport. After the airport, the road turns to dirt and crosses Big Wilson Stream. You will soon arrive at a rope gate with a trailer on the left. The same fee schedule described above applies at this entrance. Continue through the gate until you reach a T-intersection. Take a right at this intersection and go 4.5 miles to the take-out parking area on the left.

History:

The Gulf Hagas was first run some time in the 1980s. The first complete run, including Amuck, was in the spring of 1992 by Boyce Greer and Greg Hanlon.

Rich More takes the center route over the classic
Billings Falls, Gulf Hagas, Maine

Additional Information:

The Gulf Hagas can be a very dangerous run, due to the steepness of the river and the vertical walls in the Gorge. Both of these factors can make rescue and scouting difficult. Due to the river's appeal, it often attracts boaters who are not up to the challenge. A couple of spots of particular concern are the final slot in the rapid Jaws (which has been the site of multiple serious pins), and the ledge at the bottom of Amuck (which seems to change annually). Also, due to the depth and narrow width of the Gorge, the Gulf Hagas tends to hold ice much longer than its neighboring rivers. Large chunks of ice often overhang the river. Beware of falling ice as you paddle through. If a problem does arise in the Gorge, there is a hiking trail along the rim of the Gorge on river left. This trail is accessible from several points along the run. Toward the take-out, the trail begins to follow Gulf Hagas Brook (a tributary to the West Branch of the Pleasant) for a short distance. Cross this river and continue toward the take-out. When you get to the West Branch, you will be on river left and need to cross the river to get to your vehicle.

Notes

J.J. Valera runs Faceplant, Gulf Hagas, Maine

Massachusetts

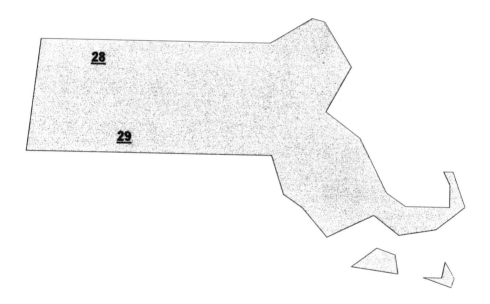

28. Dunbar Brook *
29. Hubbard Brook *

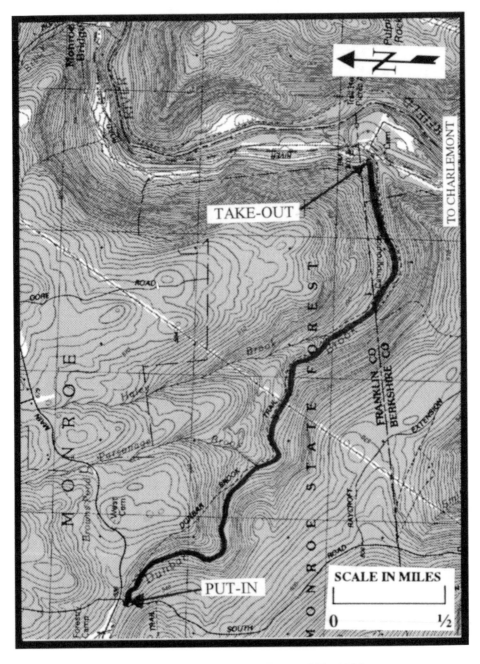

Reference Map: USGS, Rowe, MA, 1990

Image courtesy of MAPTECH, Inc.

28
Dunbar Brook *

Difficulty: Class V
Location: Granville, MA
River Miles: 2.7 miles
Average Gradient: 300 feet per mile
USGS Map: Rowe, MA
Portages: Varies

Description:

Dunbar Brook is a steep tributary of the very popular and far easier Deerfield River. The river flows southeast from Readsboro, Vermont to Monroe, Massachusetts. After passing under South Road at the put-in, Dunbar Brook drops through a beautiful, deep gorge in Monroe State Forest. No roads cross the river from the put-in to the take-out, giving the run a very remote feel. Shortly below the put-in, Dunbar Brook passes under a small foot/snowmobile bridge, marking the first significant rapid. This very steep drop, which can be scouted by beaching on a mid-stream rock ledge, is somewhat representative of what will be encountered downstream. If this is not what you had in mind for the day, it might be wise to hike back to the put-in, or plan on several portages. Below this rapid the run is continuous, increasing and decreasing in difficulty, until a set of powerlines. The powerlines mark the halfway point of the run, and the start of a long, steep rapid/portage. Scout or portage the rapid on river left, following the Dunbar Brook Trail. Another option, rather than taking the trail, would be to scout along the river's edge. This provides a better view of the rapid and the access to put in when the rapid seems more reasonable. Take out river right, just above the dam on Dunbar Brook, near the confluence with the Deerfield River. At the take out, the riverbank is very steep and sometimes difficult to manage. Use the short, wooden walkway/path from the dam to the take-out parking area.

Water Level Information:

There is no established gage on Dunbar Brook. Water level is best judged by hiking up the Dunbar Brook Trail (river right) a short distance from the take-out and looking at the final rapids. Water level can also be judged at the put-in, but be careful because the river is fairly smooth and flat here. What appears to be a moderate level at put-in, may be very high in the constricted drops downstream.

The satellite gage on the Walloomsac River in Bennington, Vermont, (Waterline #501178) can be used to estimate the general level of Dunbar Brook. Although there has been no reliable correlation developed between this gage and Dunbar, it may indicate its rising or falling tendency. A level of 3.5 feet (660 cfs) on the Walloomsac seems to correspond to somewhat high water on Dunbar Brook. Judgement must be used with this correlation, as the watershed of the Walloomsac is much larger than that of Dunbar Brook. The water level of Dunbar will usually rise and fall faster than the Walloomsac gage may indicate. The Walloomsac gage is satellite-linked and available via Waterline over the Internet.

Shuttle:

To get to the put-in from Route 2 West (Mohawk Trail) in Charlemont, Massachusetts, take a right on Zoar Road just before crossing the Deerfield River. Follow this road approximately 2.5 miles to a T-intersection. Take a left at this intersection onto River Road, and immediately pass under a railroad tressel. Continue along this road, which will take you up the beautiful Deerfield River Valley, approximately 10.5 miles to the town of Monroe Bridge, Massachusetts.

Take a left up Kingsley Hill Road, a steep hill, and go about 1.3 miles to a T-intersection at Main Road. Go left and follow Main Road approximately 2.0 miles to a left on South Road. South Road crosses Dunbar Brook shortly after this turn. Put in here. To get to the take-out, back track to the town of Monroe Bridge and take a right on River Road. Continue approximately 1.6 miles to a parking area on your right at the confluence of Dunbar Brook and the Deerfield River. From this lot you can see the dam at the Dunbar Brook take-out.

History: Unknown.

Additional Information:

Dunbar Brook seems to collect its share of logs. Beware! The Dunbar Brook Trail parallels the river off and on for the entire length of the run. The trail is on river left throughout the upper portion of the run. It then crosses to the right for lower third of the run. This trail can provide convenient access to the put-in or take-out if there are any problems on the river. Also, there is an established camping area along the trial approximately 0.75 mile from the take-out.

Notes

29
Hubbard Brook *

Difficulty: Class V
Location: Monroe, MA
River Miles: 3.7 miles
Average Gradient: 130 feet per mile
USGS Map: Southwick, MA
Portages: 0

Description:

Massachusetts is not exactly known for its wealth of steep creeks; however, Hubbard Brook provides paddlers of this area with a high-quality creek without the long drive to New Hampshire, Maine, or Vermont. Hubbard flows south from Massachusetts into Connecticut through Granville State Forest. It drains Noyes Pond, which lies above the put-in, into Barkhamsted Reservoir, just below the take-out. The riverbed consists of bedrock ledges and boulders, which form a variety of interesting rapids. Shortly below the put-in, the rapids begin before passing under West Hartland Road in Granville State Forest. Below the bridge are the best rapids, including two noteworthy ledge drops. The larger ledge drop Michaud Falls divides around a huge boulder and is the biggest drop on the run. The best line follows the flow to the right. Many more drops lead to the take-out at the USGS gaging station, river left, just above Barkhamsted Reservoir. Take out here and follow the road downstream to Route 20. You cannot paddle to Route 20 because of a dam in the river.

Water Level Information:

There is no reliable remote indicator of the level of Hubbard Brook. The USGS gage at the take-out does, however, provide an accurate measure of its level. Boaters commonly reference the concrete platform at the base of the gage house. Levels of 6 inches below the platform and even with the platform indicate low and medium levels respectively. A level of 6 inches above the platform would be considered high. Barkhamsted Reservoir, just below the gage house, is operated by the Connecticut MDC for water supply purposes. Do not paddle into the reservoir. The New Boston Gage on the Farmington River (Waterline # 251279) can provide general information about water level trends in the area. This gage is available via Waterline and over the Internet.

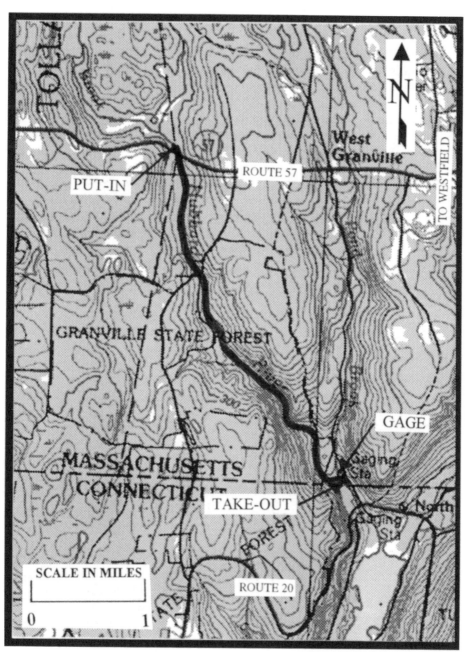

Reference Map: USGS, Southwick, MA, 1987
Image courtesy of MAPTECH, Inc.

Shuttle:

To get to the put-in from Westfield, Massachusetts, take Route 202 south to Route 57 west. Follow Route 57 through Granville and West Granville. About eleven miles from Route 202, Route 57 crosses Hubbard Brook. Park in the pull-off just after crossing the river and put in here. To get to the take-out, go east on Route 57 and take your first right onto West Hartland Road toward Granville State Forest. Continue through the State Forest, crossing Hubbard Brook to Route 20. Turn left on Route 20 west and continue until it crosses Hubbard Brook. Just after the brook is a gated road on the left, which follows Hubbard Brook upstream. The take-out is just up this road, by the USGS gaging station.

History: Unknown.

Notes

_____

_____

_____

_____

_____

_____

_____

_____

_____

_____

_____

_____

_____

_____

_____

_____

_____

Appendix

Author Greg Hanlon

Other Rivers

New England has many rivers which have yet to be scouted or paddled. Below is a list of rivers that you might be interested in exploring. Many of these have been run in part or in whole, but are not popular nor well documented.

New Hampshire:

Ellis River, Jackson, NH
Wildcat Brook, Jackson, NH
East Branch of the Saco, Bartlett, NH
Skookumchuck, Franconia, NH
Lost River, Woodstock, NH
Wild River, Beans Purchase, NH
Cockermouth River, Groton, NH

Vermont:

Borne Brook, Manchester, VT
North River (Halifax Gorge), Halifax, VT
Nulhegan River, Bloomfield, VT
North Branch of the Lamoille River, Waterville, VT
Gihon River, Johnson, VT
North Branch of the Black River, Reading, VT

Maine:

Pleasant Pond Stream, Caratunk, ME
Katahdin Stream, Baxter State Park, ME
South Branch of the Carrabassett River, Carrabassett, ME
West Branch of the Piscataquis River, Blanchard/Shirley, ME
Big Wilson Stream, Greenville, ME
Bear River, Grafton, ME

Massachusetts:

Black Brook, Savoy, MA
Lawrence Brook (Doane Falls), Royalston, MA

Connecticut:

Kent Falls Brook, Kent, CT

Boyce Greer entering The Pool, Upper Pemigewasset River, New Hampshire

River Classification

The ICF whitewater rating system assists paddlers in judging the difficulty of a run, but this scale should not be a substitute for your own judgement.

Class I

Moving water with few riffles and small waves; clear passages with few or no obstructions.

Class II

Easy rapids with waves up to three feet and wide, clear channels that are obvious without scouting. Some maneuvering is required around obvious obstacles.

Class III

Rapids with high, irregular waves capable of swamping an open canoe and narrow channels, rocks, and holes that often require complex maneuvering. May require scouting from shore.

Class IV

Long, turbulent rapids with powerful waves, holes, and constricted passages that often require precise, expert maneuvering. Scouting from shore is often necessary, and conditions make rescue difficult. Generally not possible for open canoes. Boaters in covered canoes and kayaks should be able to Eskimo roll.

Class V

Extremely difficult, long and very violent rapids with highly congested routes which nearly always must be scouted from shore. Rescue conditions are difficult and there is significant hazard to life in the event of a mishap. Ability to Eskimo Roll is essential for kayaks and canoes.

Class VI

The difficulties of Class V carried to the extreme of navigability, including irregular currents and horrendous holes. Nearly impossible and very dangerous. For teams of experts only, after close study and with all precautions taken. Generally considered *unrunnable*.

SATELLITE GAGE RATING TABLES

	Saco River @ Conway, NH	Pemi. River @ Woodstock, NH	East Branch Pemi. River @ Lincoln, NH	Contoocook River @ Henniker, NH	Baker River @ Rumney, NH
DRAINAGE AREA (sq. miles)	385	193	115	368	143
STAGE (feet)	FLOW (cfs)	FLOW (cfs)	FLOW (cfs)	FLOW (cfs)	FLOW (cfs)
1.00					96
1.50			48		232
2.00	116	37	152		430
2.50	246	136	356		664
3.00	452	330	640		946
3.50	761	583	1,090		1,256
4.00	1,150	900	1,670		1,610
4.50	1,630	1,290	2,400	64	1,982
5.00	2,270	1,750	3,350	139	2,390
5.50	3,020	2,310	4,520	245	2,801
6.00	3,890	2,960	5,900	367	3,240
6.50	4,840	3,650	7,360	510	3,675
7.00	6,020	4,420	9,000	730	4,130
7.50	7,330	5,430	10,900	1,000	4,605
8.00	8,790	6,570	13,000	1,333	5,100
8.50	10,400	7,960	15,300	1,730	5,579
9.00	12,200	9,520	17,800	2,288	6,072
9.50	14,200	11,300	20,600	2,960	6,579
10.00	16,300	13,200	23,500	3,761	7,100
10.50	18,500	15,200	26,700	4,673	7,580
11.00	20,600	17,470	30,100	5,600	8,068
11.50	22,800	19,880		6,600	8,565
12.00	24,800	22,500		7,520	9,069
12.50	26,900	24,920		8,476	9,581
13.00	29,000	27,470		9,475	10,100
13.50	31,300	30,170		10,500	10,640
14.00	33,600	33,010			11,180
14.50	35,700	36,000			11,740
15.00	37,900	39,200			12,300
15.50	40,000	42,590			13,000
16.00	42,200	46,140			13,470

SATELLITE GAGE RATING TABLES

	Smith River @ Bristol, NH	Walloomsac River @ Bennington, VT	New Haven River @ Middlebury, VT	Piscataquis River @ Blanchard, ME	Bearcamp River @ South Tamworth, NH
DRAINAGE AREA (sq. miles)	86	111	115	118	68
STAGE (feet)	FLOW (cfs)	FLOW (cfs)	FLOW (cfs)	FLOW (cfs)	FLOW (cfs)
1.00					
1.50	15	20			
2.00	36	107			
2.50	69	254	21		
3.00	130	435	70		5
3.50	230	660	139	9	22
4.00	390	920	242	40	65
4.50	620	1,220	397	110	160
5.00	870	1,550	588	225	335
5.50	1,100	1,910	830	400	620
6.00	1,350	2,300	1,130	637	1,100
6.50	1,593	2,710	1,480	936	1,800
7.00	1,850	3,150	1,890	1,320	2,400
7.50	2,114	3,590	2,360	1,790	2,950
8.00	2,397	4,060	2,869	2,200	3,550
8.50	2,700	4,540	3,435	2,500	4,270
9.00	3,007	5,040	4,060	2,780	5,070
9.50	3,316	5,560	4,753	2,970	5,900
10.00	3,615	6,100	5,510	3,200	6,800
10.50		6,650	6,332	3,390	
11.00			7,220		
11.50					
12.00					
12.50					
13.00					
13.50					
14.00					
14.50					
15.00					
15.50					
16.00					

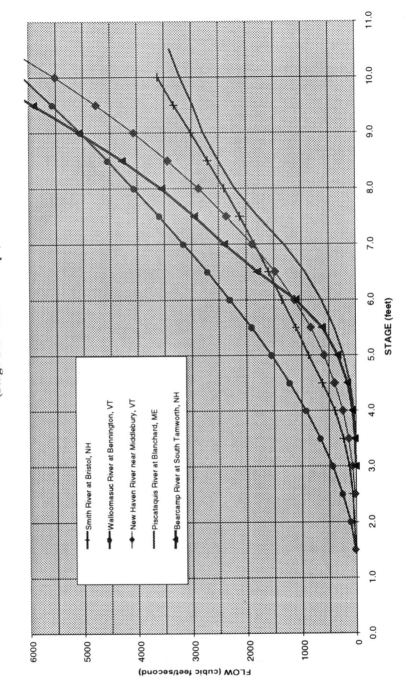

SATELLITE GAGE RATING CURVES
(Stage-Flow Relationships)

FLOW (cubic feet/second)

STAGE (feet)

— Smith River at Bristol, NH
— Walloomasuc River at Bennington, VT
— New Haven River near Middlebury, VT
— Piscataquis River at Blanchard, ME
— Bearcamp River at South Tamworth, NH

126

SATELLITE GAGE RATING CURVES
(Stage-Flow Relationships)

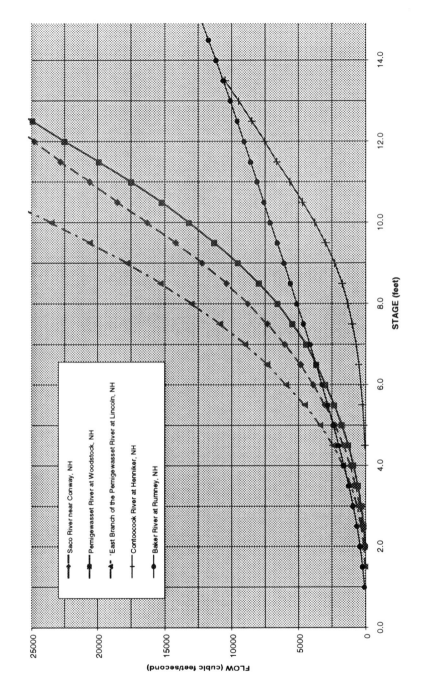

MONTHLY STREAMFLOW

	Pemigewasset River at Woodstock, NH Record 39 yrs. Thru 1977			East Branch of Pemigewasset River at Lincoln, NH Record 5 yrs. Thru 1997			Smith River at Bristol, NH Record 80 yrs. Thru 1997		
	Mean (cfs)	Maximum (cfs)	Minimun (cfs)	Mean (cfs)	Maximum (cfs)	Minimum (cfs)	Mean (cfs)	Maximum (cfs)	Minimun (cfs)
January	248	671	56	312	564	115	102	300	19
February	213	670	57	184	389	90	98	578	21
March	432	1699	66	190	254	95	249	1242	30
April	* 1320	2080	554	786	1093	264	486	1077	134
May	* 1380	2448	403	797	1323	412	227	504	72
June	496	1263	159	302	458	180	101	353	21
July	265	668	95	228	525	105	54	387	9
August	204	574	76	145	167	124	37	340	4
September	257	1212	64	123	193	68	40	457	8
October	366	1192	66	393	740	147	74	280	8
November	551	1429	122	427	760	139	131	379	25
December	422	1693	78	286	508	122	135	393	22
Annual	513	703	335	361	507	202	144	240	65

* Mean monthly flow indicates low but runnable levels on both the Upper Pemigewasset River and Cascade Brook.

MONTHLY STREAMFLOW

	Contoocook River at Henniker, NH (Record 39 yrs. Thru 1977)			Baker River at Rumney, NH (Record 50 yrs. Thru 1994)			Saco River at Conway, NH (Record 76 yrs. Thru 1997)		
	Mean (cfs)	Maximum (cfs)	Minimum (cfs)	Mean (cfs)	Maximum (cfs)	Minimum (cfs)	Mean (cfs)	Maximum (cfs)	Minimum (cfs)
January	536	1495	109	153	434	26	578	1887	144
February	566	1598	131	133	402	38	512	3170	124
March	1080	2427	172	363	2473	53	943	5986	146
April	1923	3960	647	* 874	1575	390	2624	4564	871
May	958	1962	312	464	962	141	2256	4609	614
June	487	1274	87	196	619	47	815	2189	300
July	218	837	58	103	519	22	433	2043	159
August	176	551	52	73	325	19	361	1685	129
September	211	1002	54	93	816	18	382	1794	102
October	271	1317	54	141	588	18	640	2369	114
November	532	1630	72	237	739	59	946	2493	211
December	632	1735	156	222	714	35	767	2656	152
Annual	631	1004	202	254	388	121	941	1463	489

* Mean monthly flow indicates a low but runnable level on the South Branch of the Baker River.

MONTHLY STREAMFLOW

	Bearcamp River at South Tamworth, NH (Record 5 yrs. Thru 1997)			Wallomsac River at Bennington, VT (Record 67 yrs. Thru 1997)			New Haven River at Brooksville, VT (Record 8 yrs. Thru 1997)		
	Mean (cfs)	Maximum (cfs)	Minimum (cfs)	Mean (cfs)	Maximum (cfs)	Minimum (cfs)	Mean (cfs)	Maximum (cfs)	Minimun (cfs)
January	208	331	55	193	425	62	183	386	101
February	151	284	51	181	575	54	110	188	46
March	169	257	88	320	958	68	254	494	146
April	505	632	130	* 540	1008	215	447	763	182
May	214	399	77	327	742	116	287	592	126
June	65	94	47	176	414	53	130	212	51
July	64	178	17	122	311	40	98	276	45
August	33	52	19	104	481	41	109	245	49
September	26	47	10	116	585	26	86	132	48
October	140	258	42	151	418	31	191	409	86
November	182	302	66	211	416	40	209	369	108
December	205	416	62	215	471	95	209	398	99
Annual	170	217	95	221	362	99	197	265	129

* Mean monthly flow indicates a medium level on the West Branch of the Deerfield River.

Ron Rathnow, Michaud Falls, Hubbard Brook, Massachusetts

CORRELATION NOTES

River	Gage	Level	Date/Time	Tendency	Reference River	Gage	Level	Date/Time	Tendency
Pemigewasset	abutment footing	1" above	5/16/95 12:00 p.m.	Falling	Pemigewasset	Woodstock	1350 cfs	5/16/95 12:00 p.m.	falling
					Sawyer	none	too low	5/16/95 12:00 p.m.	falling

CORRELATION NOTES

River	Gage	Level	Date/Time	Tendency	Reference River	Gage	Level	Date/Time	Tendency

CORRELATION NOTES

River	Gage	Level	Date/Time	Tendency	Reference River	Gage	Level	Date/Time	Tendency

CORRELATION NOTES

River	Gage	Level	Date/Time	Tendency	Reference River	Gage	Level	Date/Time	Tendency

138

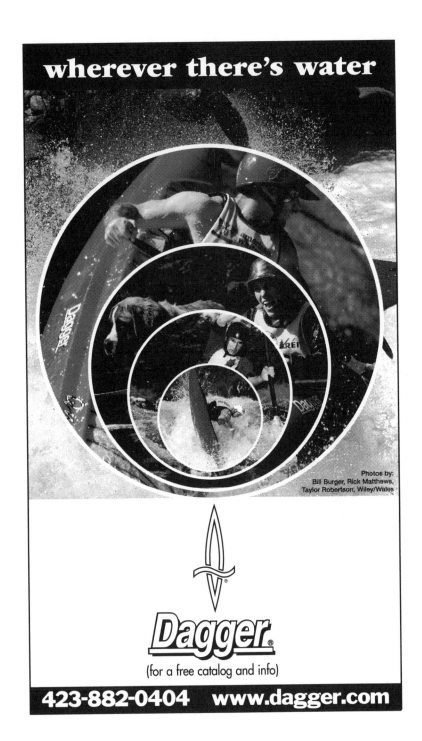

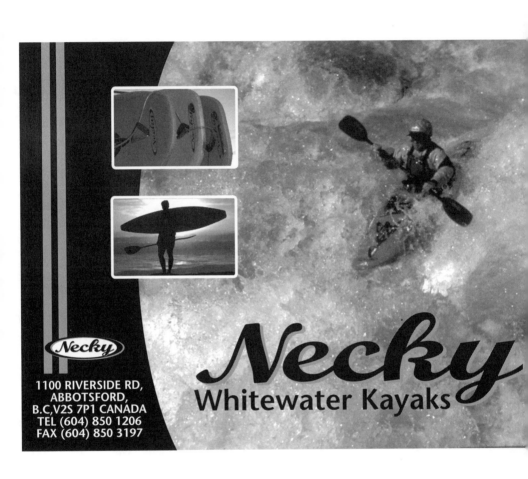
142

New England Cartographics
Price List

Maps

Holyoke Range State Park (Eastern Section)	$3.95
Holyoke Range/Skinner State Park (Western)	$3.95
Mt. Greylock Reservation Trail Map	$3.95
Mt. Toby Reservation Trail Map	$3.95
Mt. Tom Reservation Trail Map	$3.95
Mt. Wachusett and Leominster State Forest Trail Map	$3.95
Western Massachusetts Trail Map Pack (all 6 above)	$14.95
Quabbin Reservation Guide	$4.95
Quabbin Reservation Guide (waterproof version)	$5.95
New England Trails (general locator map)	$2.00
Grand Monadnock Trail Map	$3.95
Connecticut River Map (in Massachusetts)	$5.95

Books

Guide to the Metacomet-Monadnock Trail	$8.95
Hiking the Pioneer Valley	$10.95
Skiing the Pioneer Valley	$10.95
Bicycling the Pioneer Valley	$10.95
Hiking the Monadnock Region	$10.95
High Peaks of the Northeast	$12.95
Golfing in New England	$16.95
24 Great Rail-Trails of New Jersey	$16.95
Steep Creeks of New England	$14.95

Please include postage/handling:
$0.75 for the first single map and $0.25 for each additional map;
$1.00 for the Western Mass. Map Pack; $2.00 for the first book
and $1.00 for each additional book.

Postage/Handling _____

Total Enclosed_____

Order Form

To order, call or write:
New England Cartographics
P.O. Box 9369, North Amherst MA 01059
(413) 549-4124
FAX orders: (413) 549-3621
Toll-Free (888) 995-6277 (Outside 413 Area Code)

Circle one: Mastercard   Visa   Amex   Check

Card Number_____

Expiration Date _____

Signature_____

Telephone (optional) _____

Please send my order to:

Name _____

Address _____

_____

Town/City _____

State _____ **Zip** _____